C000173112

TRIGGERED LITERATURE

TRIGGERED LITERATURE

Cancellation, Stealth Censorship and Cultural Warfare

JOHN SUTHERLAND

Biteback Publishing

First published in Great Britain in 2023 by
Biteback Publishing Ltd, London
Copyright © John Sutherland 2023

ISBN 978-1-78590-817-0

10 9 8 7 6 5 4 3 2 1

A CIP catalogue record for this book is available from the British Library.

Set in Minion Pro and Bebas Neue

Printed and bound in Great Britain by
CPI Group (UK) Ltd, Croydon CR0 4YY

FSC
www.fsc.org
MIX
Paper | Supporting
responsible forestry
FSC® C171272

'We each have our little triggers.'
NEIL GAIMAN, *TRIGGER WARNING*

'Altogether, I think we ought to read only books that bite and sting us. If the book does not shake us awake like a blow to the skull, why bother reading it in the first place? So that it can make us happy, as you put it? Good God, we'd be just as happy if we had no books at all ... What we need are books that hit us like a most painful misfortune, like the death of someone we loved more than ourselves, that make us feel as though we had been banished to the woods, far from any human presence, like a suicide. A book must be the axe for the frozen sea within us.'
FRANZ KAFKA

CONTENTS

AUTHOR'S NOTE

I preface what follows with a trigger warning. This book contains reference, quotation and content discussion of what some may find disturbing material. The warning is not ironic. Some of what follows disturbs me.

Much of what was banned in the past revolved around 'four-letter words', notably a word beginning with 'F'. Much of modern triggering, erasure and cancellation revolves around a word beginning with 'N'. In discussion where an author uses the word 'nigger', I have retained it. Where I use the word, I have asterisked it as 'n***er'. I have made every effort in the text under my control, not quotation, to avoid offensiveness.

This book, I may add, has not been subjected to any 'sensitivity reading' other than that routine in the editorial process.

Many of the trigger points for what follows have been publicised by what is loosely called the 'right-wing press' – the *Daily* and *Sunday Telegraph*, the *Daily Mail* and *The Times*. Although I have a more mixed mind on the matter, I appreciate the valuable light they have thrown on an important topic.

PREFACE

The topic addressed in this book is, loosely, current controls on literary culture in its many evolving forms. Nominally triggering is the subject along with a range of other impositions on the creative act and product: namely, cancellation, prepublication bowdlerisation, suppression, 'red flagging', semi-tolerance. Burning in any other than a metaphorical or theatrical sense is nowadays rare. But even in literary cultures, like those of the English-speaking world, which boast their freedom of expression, extra-literary control exists at points from the moment of creation (inspiration), gestation (editorial revision), delivery (publication), distribution and consumption. And, nowadays, in comes the 'sensitivity reader'. Creative literature's superego.

The account which follows begins with a survey of the arrival and rapid evolution of triggering and other 'warning' mechanisms: thumbs in the literary pudding and pie.

The Introduction is followed by a section of brief items (500 words or less) presented as 'Signs of the Times'. They compose a *pointilliste* picture, without comment, of where we are and where we're going.

Thereafter, comes a section, 'Machineries', anatomising larger and pervasive mechanisms of creation, production, distribution, reception, consumption and, in all of them, new forms of control on the literary product.

The third section, 'Case Studies', comprises extended single-case, free-range meditations on triggered works. The book ends with a self-reflective Epilogue.

INTRODUCTION

'Triggering' was, one fancies, a candidate for the *Oxford English Dictionary*'s 'Word of the Year' in 2014 ('vape' won). When and where did the usage originate? No one is sure. There is, however, clear connection with the psychiatric term 'trauma trigger' – stimuli which can detonate unhealed wounds. The clinical term was in the air after the Vietnam War in the treatment of American veterans with PTSD (post-traumatic stress disorder).

The concept of triggering printed and e-circulated text took off in feminist magazines and social media 'chat' around 2010. *Ms Magazine*, *Spare Rib* and LiveJournal are cited as early adopters. Anything coming which might retraumatise susceptible readers was 'triggered'. 'Here be Dragons' as old maps (supposedly) used to warn. 'Trigger warning' entered common use at the same period as the premonitory 'spoiler alerts' were being used for films and literature whose effects depend on surprise or shock. It amounted to 'prepping' the reader.

There was demographic force behind the triggering of literature. Women and minorities had been, after long suppression and downright oppression, more proportionately recruited into opinion-forming outlets – publishing, journalism, broadcasting – at decision-making not service (coffee-fetching, jiffy-bag-stuffing, short-hand typing, mailroom) level. Once aboard, they were no longer servile. Levers were in their hands.

There were early signs. It was furious middle-rank female employees who strong-armed Simon & Schuster into junking *American Psycho* (costing the firm hundreds of thousands of dollars in advances paid and compensation) after the proofs of Bret Easton Ellis's graphically gynophobic (ironically, he claims) novel circulated in-house in 1990.

Around 2013–14, triggering moved, wholesale, into higher education. Again, infrastructural shift laid the way. In humanities disciplines (literature, history, philosophy), women had generally achieved numerical parity at staff, research and student levels. Science subjects, patriarchal to the last test tube, put up fierce resistance before falling.

Triggering among women writing for women received lateral impetus from the #MeToo insurgency and its witness that there was more sexual abuse in society than had previously been supposed, exposed or dealt with. The Black Lives Matter movement made its own assertion about oppression of African Americans. It was allied with another acronym, 'CRT' – critical race theory (implication: 'you're racist but don't realise it'). In post-imperial Britain, 'decolonising the curriculum' was a parallel rallying call (implication: 'you're post-imperialist but don't realise it').

Fifty years after historical decolonisation, Harold Macmillan's winds of change were whipping round the dreaming towers of his alma mater Oxford strongly enough to shake but not topple the statue of Cecil Rhodes – the magnate who believed the greatest thing God could give to man was to be Anglo-Saxon. The second greatest thing was to own Africa.

The 1964 Civil Rights Act in the US and the 1967 Sexual Offences Act and the 2006 Gender Recognition Act in the UK, as well as post-colonial immigration into a newly polycultural Britain, had widened the ethnic composition and sexualities of student populations in the English-speaking world. Optimists saw it as 'rainbowism'. Change it certainly was.

Over the same period, the whopping cost of fees had transformed the higher education UK and US student body into customers wielding the big bazooka: purchaser power. Proverbially, 'the customer is always right'. Students were by the second decade of the twenty-first century customers, not begowned ephebes or acolytes. Student money talked. The university listened. Curricular power switched. With the switch it became clear, interestingly, that young people were a different kind of reader from their elders. They largely read what they read on different sites. The iPhone and lectern were generations and planets apart. It was fast food versus sit-down dining.

In May 2014, the *New York Times* reported, with a gasp of surprise, that at scores of institutions – from Ivy Leagues to community colleges – student bodies were demanding trigger warnings in their courses for canonical texts such as *Things Fall Apart* by Chinua Achebe, *The Great Gatsby* by F. Scott Fitzgerald, *Mrs Dalloway* by Virginia Woolf and *The Merchant of Venice* by William Shakespeare. Where had all that come from? 'Follow the Money' as 'Deep Throat' told Bernstein and Woodward.

The student demands for triggers were made on behalf of 'readers who have experienced racism, colonialism, religious persecution, violence, suicide and more'. The tail wagged the dog. Such was current student financial muscle that triggering was duly installed in the US at college level as 'responsible pedagogical practice'. It was, more honestly, what in chess is called 'a forced move'.

For school children and infants, the content warnings were directed by similarly 'responsible' publishers and websites at teachers and parents (e.g. Parent Previews, Trigger Warning Database and Moms for Liberty). Here too was a generational difference: tots had not taken over the kindergarten curriculum or the TV remote control. But a pattern was set from above where subtle power exchanges were taking place. Without fanfare, or public notice, bloodthirsty classics like 'Little Red Riding Hood' (poor, wolf-snack, granny) slid off the shelf into bedtime nonentity. The Great Reform in children's reading ('Up with Dahl! Down with Dahl!') is discussed in the following pages. It is part of a larger pattern.

A poll of 800 American college teachers in 2016 revealed that half of those surveyed had issued student-impelled trigger warnings on taught materials in humanities courses. There was also content origin complaints to act on. Where were the multi-ethnic writers, philosophers, scientists? By the third decade of the century, triggering and 'curriculum cultural spread' were on the way to being universal 'good practice'. Literature now came into the seminar locked and loaded. And a quantity of it triggered.

On being informed in 2014 of what was going on in America by *The Guardian*, John Mullan, the head of English studies at UCL, retorted dismissively that triggering was 'treating people as if they are babies, and studying literature is for grownups at university'.

There was a cheering chorus of 'hear, hear!' from those who saw themselves as grown(er) up(er) than fractious students with weak knees. But the tide was with youth. It reached a floodmark with a survey by *The Times* in August 2022 which found, via freedom of information requests, that British universities had covertly triggered over a thousand texts, including the work of literary greats such as 'William Shakespeare, Geoffrey Chaucer, Jane Austen, Charlotte Brontë, Charles Dickens and Agatha Christie'.

The *Scottish Daily Express* did its own FOI survey in August 2022 of Scottish universities. Among its 'catch' was that the University of the Highlands and Islands had triggered Ernest Hemingway's *The Old Man and the Sea*, on the grounds of 'graphic fishing scenes'. I shall never eat a Stornoway kipper, or an Arbroath smokie, again without thinking of the poor herring's pain.

Triggering was by now a hot political issue. On reading in the *Daily Mail* in January 2022 that *Harry Potter* had been triggered by Chester University,* the then British Universities Minister, Michelle Donelan, protested that '*Harry Potter* is actually a children's book. Fundamentally it is probably a multi-million-pound industry that has been franchised into films.'

It was a slightly cock-eyed but truly Tory argument that J. K. Rowling's books should be read by university students untriggered because they had made millions for United Kingdom PLC.

Donelan has a degree in history and politics from York University, a member of the 24-strong elite Russell Group. The group – as a magnet for high-paying overseas students – earns handsomely for Britain. The University of York is, as the 2020s roll on, a dedicated triggerer. The study of literature, in toto, carries the warning: 'In many cases, the language forms we will encounter in the module are taboo terms (slurs, insults, swear words, slang terms, etc.) with the potential to cause offence.'

An archaeological module on Egyptian mummies warned prospective students that they would find reference to dead bodies. It seems absurd, but the actual business of embalming is, indeed, if you look it up, stomach turning – particularly if the class is before lunch.

The minister's comment that '*Harry Potter* is actually a children's book' is dubious. Later instalments of the Potteriad are

---

* For incoming students in an 'Approaches to Literature' module. It was triggered on the grounds that it could generate 'difficult conversations about gender, race, sexuality, class, and identity.'

teen fiction, verging on adult. Questionable too is the implication that children's literature requires no triggering.

In 2021, Cambridge University's Homerton College, an
institution for the higher education of future schoolteachers,
announced that it was subjecting its huge library archive of
children's books to 'sensitivity reading', with necessary warning inscribed. The laborious exercise was part funded by an
£80,633 grant from the UK Arts and Humanities Research
Council. Big bad wolves who huffed and puffed little piggies'
houses down and giants who ground up Englishmen for their
daily bread were themselves for the chop.* Fee, fi, fo, fum.

The commonsense party airily vilifies triggering with the
sarcasms 'wokery' and 'snowflakery'. Some instances do seem
on the face of it wonky. In January 2022, in response to an FOI
request, Northampton University (motto: '*Ne Nesciamus*' –
'Let us not be ignorant') revealed that it had triggered George
Orwell's *Nineteen Eighty-Four* in a course entitled 'Identity
Under Construction'. Constructing 'identity' (notably gender
identity) was currently topical.

Students choosing the module were warned that Orwell's
novel 'addresses challenging issues related to violence, gender,
sexuality, class, race, abuses, sexual abuse, political ideas and
offensive language'.

The offensive term Orwell allowed himself in print was
'bollox'. This seems, on the face of it, to warrant, in the novel's Newspeak 'doubledoubleplusbollox'. But looked at more

---

* Homerton kept the results to themselves but it was leaked that the Dr Seuss books were triggered for 'overt blackface'. See below, pp. 203–5.

closely, Orwell's novel has uncomfortable moments. Take, for example, the fantasy Winston has when first seeing Julia at the Two Minutes Hate:

> Suddenly, by the sort of violent effort with which one wrenches one's head away from the pillow in a nightmare, Winston succeeded in transferring his hatred from the face on the screen ['Emmanuel Goldstein, the Enemy of the People'] to the dark-haired girl behind him. Vivid, beautiful hallucinations flashed through his mind. He would flog her to death with a rubber truncheon. He would tie her naked to a stake and shoot her full of arrows like Saint Sebastian. He would ravish her and cut her throat at the moment of climax.

The switch from Jew-hating to sadistic misogyny is alarming.

It is, of course, Winston Smith who has this fantasy. Whether or not Orwell was antisemitic has been a long-running, still-running, argument. The prosecution case, with multiple examples, is mounted by Richard Bradford in the *Jewish Chronicle* on 3 January 2020. His article was precipitated by what he saw as the new-Orwellian (i.e. supposedly 'non-offensive') antisemitism in the Corbyn-led Labour Party. Bradford's examination pivots on what Orwell himself said, in a 1945 essay, 'Why does antisemitism appeal to me? What is there about it that I feel to be true?' It's an extremely honest, extremely discomfiting confession for someone who was already a widely read sage to put into print.

It's topical since, at the time of writing, one can recall the first entry in Winston's diary (for a *Times* editor his punctuation is strangely shaky):

April 4th, 1984. Last night to the flicks. All war films. One very good one of a ship full of refugees being bombed … then you saw a lifeboat full of children with a helicopter hovering over it. there was a middle-aged woman might have been a jewess sitting up in the bow with a little boy about three years old in her arms. little boy screaming with fright and hiding his head between her breasts as if he was trying to burrow right into her … then the helicopter planted a 20 kilo bomb in among them terrific flash and the boat went all to matchwood. then there was a wonderful shot of a child's arm going up up up right up into the air.

This, again, is not Orwell but the as yet unregenerate Winston Smith. But, in a novel published in 1951, with the Holocaust and foundation of Israel in the world's mind, it is insensitive. I imagine any undergraduate at Northampton of Jewish heritage might well feel uneasy after studious examination of *Nineteen Eighty-Four*.

With our current PM pledging (again as I write) to 'deal with the small boats' (i.e. 'illegal' refugees), any first-generation British undergraduate whose family received asylum in Britain might be similarly uneasy.

There is no indictment intended here; I am merely pointing towards a trickiness in a great novel. Similarly tricky is the misogyny in the Two Minutes Hate. The authorised biography by Bernard Crick as well as other eye-witnesses testify to the fact that Orwell was not always safe around women, especially alone with them in open places when, the suggestion is, he was assaultive.* It's an uncomfortable topic but again makes the point that Northampton's triggering *Nineteen Eighteen-Four* was not egregious snowflakery (as the press generally took it to be) but imposed on the basis of careful, legitimately sensitive reading.

What is routinely overlooked in the heat of polemic, heated up by examples like Northampton and *Nineteen Eighty-Four*, is that triggering is categorically different from traditional institutional (religious, educational, dictatorial) controls on literature. Triggering is in essence an alert. Done responsibly it does not erase or meddle; it stimulates curiosity and thought. It honours the fact that great literature is great because it is, as Kafka says, powerful.† It should, for that reason, be handled with critical care. Like, to modify the firearm metaphor, a hand grenade with the pin pulled.

I, personally, can live with triggering if done properly. I also believe, more importantly, that triggering is a recent phenomenon of future consequence. It is not something to be pooh-poohed away. It is a significant theatre of culture warfare. Politicians, hungry for office, in the two great sectors of the English-speaking world have taken up arms in that conflict. Jonathan Swift's 'Battle of the Books' has flared up again.

---

*   I deal with this issue at some length in *Orwell's Nose: A Pathological Biography* (2016).

†   Incidentally, there are seven trigger warnings recommended for Kafka's story *Metamorphosis* on the website Book Trigger Warnings, including 'pessimistic thinking'.

The newly appointed deputy chairman of the Tory Party, Lee Anderson, put the issue with his customary bluntness: 'The big thing in terms of 2019, there were three things that won us the election. It was nothing to do with me. It was Brexit, it was Boris, it was Corbyn and it was as simple as that. Those three things together were a great campaign, great ingredients.'

That was yesterday's battle and crushing Tory victory. For 2024, Anderson forecast that a 'mix of culture wars and trans debate' would be 'at the heart' of the party's coming election campaign along with critical race theory and 'brainwashing' in schools and universities.

Newspapers (principally the *Telegraphs*, *Mails*, *Sun*, *Expresses* and more judiciously *The Times* and *Sunday Times*) supportive of the Conservative cause had already sensed where the soft underbelly of the Labour Party which Anderson talked about would be. The forces of the right (I use the phrase hyperbolically) located a main point of attack: the defence of 'classically "English" books'. Books which incarnated post-Brexit, sovereign England.

By early 2023, the strategy was cooked and ready to serve in articles, such as Richard Littlejohn's on 27 March which was headlined: 'Roald Dahl, Ian Fleming and now Agatha Christie… when are the wokerati going to stop butchering classic works of literature?'

Littlejohn continued with reference to the previous night's first instalment of the BBC adaptation of *Great Expectations*:

No author is safe from the revisionists, not even Charles

Dickens, judging by the BBC's latest adaptation of *Great Expectations* by the *Peaky Blinders'* creator Steven Knight.

Reading our TV critic Christopher Stevens's brilliant review in yesterday's *Mail* [he entitled the series 'Woke Desecrations' and gave it one star], it is blindingly apparent that this bleak production lives down to our worst expectations.

It features an opium-smoking Miss Havisham, a foul-mouthed Pip and a little light spanking as Mrs Joe – now called Sara, to prevent her being seen as a mere chattel of her husband – turns dominatrix. Not exactly 'sensitive' but utterly in line with today's warped artistic values.

Yet while drug-taking, a torrent of four-letter words, graphic sex scenes and sado-masochism sail through the 'best possible taste' barrier, far more innocent works are bowdlerised to appease the 'diversity' brigade and plastered with trigger warnings. Talk about double standards.

The Labour Party was currently introverted verging on paralytic; not yet come to terms with its deCorbynisation programme and being torn to breaking point by tensions between its radical young members (formerly Momentum) and the grizzled hands on the levers of party power, patronage and revenue (formerly Union Barons).

In the USA, also looking forward to 2024, the Governor of Florida, Ron DeSantis, the hopeful Republican presidential candidate, had devised as his wedge issue (against Trump as well as the Democrats) 'parental' rights.

Who owns your child's mind? Mom and Dad or the school

your child attends? DeSantis, his wife on his arm, daughters at his knee, asked. Centripetally, DeSantis's 'parentalism' drew in a hotpot of issues: CRT; gender fluidities; 'metropolitan' (pro-choice) vs 'homeland' (pro-life) prejudices but above all what was being imposed on young minds by school reading materials. It was, as DeSantis argued, a crisis for the soul of America: children were being brainwashed out of their home values. Higher brainwashing was going on at college level – paid for, in state colleges – by the taxpayer.

Following DeSantis's 'Stop Woke' and 'Don't Say Gay' initiatives, America in 2022 saw more books banned than ever before in its recorded history. And if/when DeSantis became the 47th President of the United States – with federal power – what then would be banned?[*]

There are contrary arguments that triggering is utter wokery, or responsible pedagogic practice. There is a third view – it's a hoax. Every student entering the University of Chicago as an undergraduate in September 2016 received the following welcome letter from the dean of students:

> Welcome and congratulations on your acceptance to the College at the University of Chicago. Earning a place in our community of scholars is no small achievement and we are delighted that you selected Chicago to continue your intellectual journey. Once here you will discover that one of the University of Chicago's defining characteristics

---

[*] For more on Governor DeSantis, see pp. 49–50, 224–8.

is our commitment to freedom of inquiry and expression ...
Our commitment to academic freedom means that we do
not support so-called 'trigger warnings', we do not cancel
invited speakers because their topics might prove controversial, and we do not condone the creation of intellectual
'safe spaces' where individuals can retreat from ideas and
perspectives at odds with their own ... Again, welcome to
the University of Chicago. See you in September!

Inspired by Chicago's fighting declaration, which received
countrywide publicity and approbation, a team of seven
psychologists and scholarly aides, under the auspices of the
National Library of Medicine, resolved to investigate experi-
mentally whether trigger warnings actually worked.

Their research and its conclusions were published in March
2021 in an article entitled 'Student reactions to traumatic material in literature: Implications for trigger warnings'.

The implications were interesting. As the report described,
355 undergraduate students from four respected universities
were invited to read a passage describing incidences of both
physical and sexual assault. Longitudinal measures of subjective distress, awakened PTSD symptoms and emotional reac-
tivity were taken at various stages.

The results were, on the face of it, decisive:

Greater than 96 per cent of participants read the triggering
passage even when given a non-triggering alternative to
read. Of those who read the triggering passage, those with

triggering traumas did not report more distress although those with higher PTSD scores did. Two weeks later, those with trigger traumas and/or PTSD did not report an increase in trauma symptoms as a result of reading the triggering passage.

The conclusions were similarly forthright: 'Students with relevant traumas do not avoid triggering material and the effects appear to be brief. Students with PTSD do not report an exacerbation of symptoms two weeks later as a function of reading the passage.'

Case closed. That triggering forestalls the incidence of trauma stress in vulnerable individuals is untrue. The practice is provenly unnecessary.

Afterthoughts arise, however, with consideration of the passage the students were exposed to that was potentially traumatising. It was the incestuous paedophile rape scene in Toni Morrison's first published novel, *The Bluest Eye* (1970). The action is set in the Depression era. Pecola is an eleven-year-old child; Cholly, the rapist, is her father; an alcoholic with a traumatic past.

The students were given a hard copy of the book. The requirement was they should read the page-assigned rape scene along with a 'neutral scene' from the novel which served as a 'control' to measure response norms.

All 355 students were in the same nineteen to twenty-one age group and all were taking an introductory psychology course at one of their four institutions. Most, one assumes, would go on in their junior (third) year to a variety of majors. They received course credit for no more than merely participating in the triggering experiment: an easy 'A' towards their grade point average. Sixty-eight per cent of total participants were female; 32 per cent male. They identified as being from a variety of majority and minority ethnic and racial backgrounds. The important numbers were 69 per cent white; 10 per cent black; 30 per cent other.

The format of the experiment was standard across the four institutions. On day one, the participants came to a lab, or classroom; there they signed a consent form and were given a pack. It included a personal questionnaire, one of the two passages ('rape' or 'neutral') and response forms. The initial reading of the scene in question lasted thirty minutes before papers were collected. Students took away the book.

As a follow-up, over the next three days, the participants received an email link and were asked to find a 'quiet place' to complete the survey within twenty-four hours. Two weeks later came a second email designed to pick up lasting effect. Finally, investigators debriefed them thoroughly.

The procedure, as an experimental process, was impeccable. There are, however, on close inspection, disturbing factors. Morrison's novel had (with her Nobel win) canonical status by 2020. Although *The Bluest Eye* was one of the most banned novels in America, many mature school pupils would have read the book or heard about it and its author.

The rape is black on black. The self-identified white/black participation ratio in the experiment, roughly 70:10, is disproportionate. The crime isolated from context could, for some participants, be seen to slander African Americans as animalic.

Morrison's narrative is carefully diagnostic of Cholly's 'tender' violation of his child. Commentary makes the point that he has internalised white prejudices about African Americans such as he. Cholly, like Pecola, is a victim of larger historical violence. The scene, taken this way, does not invite or allow sympathy – only a degree of understanding.

Equally the (roughly) similar female/male 70:30 imbalance could, one fancies, skew results. As critics have pointed out, this rape scene is unusual in that it is visualised by 'the female gaze'. It will not excite the primitive male lusts common in violation-themed pornography.

Finally, how well, it is not condescending to ask, can 355 first-year psychology students read an intricately voiced symbolically wrought work of fiction like *The Bluest Eye*? Morrison is a difficult author. Every class on her from twelfth grade to postgraduate seminar will start from that point. What, ideally, the investigating team could have done was to commission a completely fresh written, simpler, scene of violence and sexual assault – without ethnic, high literary or gender contaminants. *The Bluest Eye* comes trailing with too much baggage.

With all respect to the team who went to such lengths to test the theory and practice of triggering, the question, I believe, is still open.

But what do authors think about triggering? Most writers triggered are dead – beyond resentment or approval. Among those still with us who have voiced an opinion is Neil Gaiman, who speaks his mind (a remarkable one) in the preface to his eponymously entitled collection of short fiction, *Trigger Warning*.

He sees such 'warnings' not as fingers on the loaded firearm but unwanted fingers in his, Neil Gaiman's, pie. Such interference is, he believes, contrary to the wholly unpredictable nature (even to authors themselves) of what lies, hitherto unknown, within his head. His fiction revolves around 'the monsters in our cupboards and our minds [which] are always there in the darkness'. His art unlooses them to ravage on his pages. He does not, he says, want his readers 'groomed'. Like Kafka, he belongs to the hammer to the skull authorial party.

'I first discovered the phrase "trigger warning"', Gaiman says,

where it existed primarily to warn people of links to images or ideas that could upset them and trigger flashbacks or anxiety or terror, in order that the images or ideas could be filtered out of a feed, or that the person reading could be mentally prepared before encountering them.

I was fascinated when I learned that trigger warnings had crossed the divide from the Internet to the world of things you could touch. Several colleges, it was announced, were considering putting trigger warnings on works of literature, art or film, to warn students of what was waiting for them, an idea that I found myself simultaneously warming to (of course you want to let people who may be distressed that this might distress them) while at the same time being deeply troubled by it.

He continues: 'I wonder, *Are fictions safe places*? And then I ask myself, *Should they be safe places*?' No, he resolves, they shouldn't, adding:

I know a lady called Rocky who is upset by tentacles, and who genuinely needs warnings for things that have tentacles in them, especially tentacles with suckers, and who, confronted with an unexpected squid or octopus, will dive, shaking, behind the nearest sofa. There is an enormous tentacle somewhere in these pages. Many of those stories end badly for at least one of the people in them. Consider yourself warned.

Here be giant squids.

PART ONE

SIGNS OF THE TIMES: A CALENDAR

ALL IN A DAY

The day was 31 January 2023. That morning the *Daily Telegraph* carried an editorial noting, with wry distaste, that the University of Greenwich – having the previous year triggered Coleridge's 'The Rime of the Ancient Mariner' on the grounds of 'animal death' and 'supernatural possession' – had triggered Jane Austen's *Northanger Abbey* on the grounds of 'toxic relations and friendships'. On the same day, *The Guardian* carried a front-page story headlined 'One in 10 children "have watched pornography by the time they are nine"'.

According to a report by the Children's Commissioner for England, the figure had risen to a quarter of the cohort by the time they left primary school. And 'four out of five of those surveyed have seen pornography involving violence by the age of 18 … Nearly half of the male 16- to 21-year-olds who took part in the survey assumed girls either "expect" or "enjoy" sex which involves physical aggression, such as airway restriction.'

'Airway restriction' means erotic strangulation.

On the same day, *The Times* reported the fact that 'Kevin Anderson & Associates, a company that supplies sensitivity readers, says its "cultural accuracy editing" will "ensure your manuscript isn't offensive, inaccurate or perpetuating harmful stereotypes"'.

HAMLET: THE ANDREW TATE VERSION*

On 15 April 2023, the *Daily Mail* warned its readers that a forthcoming BBC programme 'has been commissioned to mark 400 years since the publication of the Bard's First Folio'. Well and good. The Folio was being touted as the most important British book since the King James Bible. Anything but good was that an 'Oxford professor', the series presenter, would argue that 'Hamlet is a misogynist like Andrew Tate'.

The 'Oxford professor' was Emma Smith. Her declared aim was to 'reexamine the works of the Bard through a modern lens'. What that optic would reveal was that Hamlet is the embodiment of

'toxic masculinity' like the 'alpha male' influencer Andrew Tate, who is reportedly being sued by three women in the UK for rape and sexual assault ... In the series, the host will challenge celebrity guests to look at the playwright's work

---

* Nahum Tate famously reversioned *King Lear* to excise its horrors and give the play a happy ending; Dr Johnson preferred Tate's *Lear*. Professor Smith in what follows is inclined to reverse the process and make *Hamlet* more horrific.

differently, speaking to the likes of Gordon Brown about Julius Caesar.

'Alpha male' is too flattering. As Shanti Das described him in *The Guardian* on 6 August 2022:

> Andrew Tate says women belong in the home, can't drive, and are a man's property.
>
> He also thinks rape victims must 'bear responsibility' for their attacks and dates women aged 18–19 because he can 'make an imprint' on them, according to videos posted online.
>
> In other clips, the British-American kickboxer – who poses with fast cars, guns and portrays himself as a cigar-smoking playboy – talks about hitting and choking women, trashing their belongings and stopping them from going out.
>
> 'It's bang out the machete, boom in her face and grip her by the neck. Shut up bitch,' he says in one video.

Hard to square, perhaps, with Ophelia's eulogy:

> O, what a noble mind is here o'erthrown!
> The courtier's, soldier's, scholar's, eye, tongue, sword;
> The expectancy and rose of the fair state,
> The glass of fashion and the mould of form,
> The observed of all observers.

Only the last line fits Andrew Tate. He had 4.6 million 'observers', so to call them, on Instagram before being banned.

Professor Smith would use her programme, it was forecast, to persuade the witty contrarian Will Self of her case. As she put it: 'Talking about toxic masculinity and Hamlet, we can see him as a young man radicalised, on a mission to clear things up, and turning against women's sexuality in a very violent way, maybe like the guy who takes a gun to school … That was revelatory for me.'

Revelatory too for most critics before Professor Smith.

Seeing Hamlet as kin to an American school spree shooter is a very dark new lens. It is true, though, that Hamlet's personal murder count in the course of the play – five or more – is high. And Professor Smith does make us ponder whether he is Shakespeare's John Wick.*

Andrew Tate, who lives on TikTok (when not languishing in a Romanian prison on sex trafficking charges), has not commented, at the time of writing, on his being Hamletised.

UNIVERSAL DARKNESS COVERS ALL

On 23 January 2023, the *Washington Post* (motto 'Democracy Dies in Darkness') reported:

Students arrived in some Florida public school classrooms this month to find their teachers' bookshelves wrapped in paper – or entirely barren of books – after district officials

---

* In April 2023 one of the films doing best at the cinema and on stream was *John Wick: Chapter 4*. Fans estimate that Wick's (played frozen-faced by Keanu Reeves) body count is 439; the remorseless slaughter is in revenge for gangsters killing his beloved beagle Daisy.

launched a review of the texts' appropriateness under a new state law [Florida House Bill 1467, which] ... mandates that schools' books be age-appropriate, free from pornography and 'suited to student needs.' Books must be approved by a qualified school media specialist, who must undergo a state retraining on book collection. The Education Department did not publish that training until January, leaving school librarians across Florida unable to order books for more than a year.

The new law comes atop an older one that makes distributing 'harmful materials' to minors, including obscene and pornographic materials, a third-degree felony – meaning that a teacher could face up to five years in prison and a $5,000 fine, a spokeswoman from the Florida Department of Education said Tuesday.

ALL CHANGE

The *London Evening Standard* reported on 20 April 2023 that

a leading London private school has overhauled its English curriculum to introduce a diverse range of authors and challenge 'white-centric, patriarchal and cis-gender ideologies'.

Pupils at the £25,000-a-year Alleyn's School in Dulwich now discuss Macbeth's toxic masculinity and read *The Tempest* through the lens of colonialism. Sixth formers study 'queer readings' of A-level texts such as *Dracula*, and the first text by a non-binary author has been included in the

A-level curriculum. Half of the books read by students in years seven, eight and nine are by female authors, which 'helps in some way to counteract the lack of equality in the set texts for GCSE'.

A-level students must also choose one coursework text by a writer of colour 'in an effort to tackle the lack of diversity in the A-level syllabus'.

An educational 'all change'? Or overdue reform?

Alex Smith, head of English studies at Alleyn's, complained that the same old texts – *Macbeth*, *Lord of the Flies*, *Of Mice and Men* and *To Kill a Mockingbird* for example – have been 'wheeled out time and time again' for decades, propping up a 'pale, male and stale' reading list. No more geriatric books in wheelchairs for the school's coeducational classes.

Writing on the school blog, Smith stated its mission:

For the last five years, the Alleyn's English department have been committed to a thorough and ongoing overhaul and genuine diversification of our English curriculum in the hope that every child will come to see themselves, and the rich and varied world around them, represented in the texts they study and that, by doing so, they will be equipped with the empathy and confidence to challenge and dismantle sexism, racism, homophobia – indeed, discrimination of any kind – when they encounter it.

She announced that the school has changed the way pupils

would henceforth study canonical texts by 'white, cis-male authors' to challenge 'white-centric, patriarchal, and cisgender ideologies'. Colonialism was high on the list. 'We are also committed', said Smith, 'to representing alternative versions of masculinity to those harmful tropes so often seen perpetuated in popular culture and by the media. The toxicity of Macbeth's masculinity – and, crucially, its consequences – is central to our study of that text at GCSE.'

Smith's statistical foundation was a report by the campaign group 'End Sexism in Schools', which had found that 77 per cent of novels studied by pupils in years seven, eight and nine are written by men, and 82 per cent of them have male protagonists. The group said that 99 per cent of plays taught to students in these year groups were by male writers. Exeunt omnes.

GOOD GOLLY, MISS MOLLY*

On 9 April 2023, the *Daily Mail* reported, with barely concealed mirth, that 'the Home Secretary has scolded a police force for sending five officers to a family-owned pub to seize a collection of golliwog dolls'.

A couple of weeks earlier, an anonymous complaint had been made against the White Hart Inn in Grays, Essex, and fifteen dolls were duly seized on suspicion of a 'hate crime'. Talk shows, particularly Nick Ferrari (an LBC host senior

---

* Apologies to Little Richard and the Beatles.

politicians pay much attention to) had gone to town on the raid. A SWAT team for dolls? What next? Speeding offences for Dinky cars? The Home Secretary, Suella Braverman, surfing the furore, told Essex Police, sharply, to focus on catching real criminals not on seizing toys.

Co-owner of the White Hart, Benice Ryley, after being questioned, said she would put up a warning sign. Her fifteen dolls remained confiscated as evidence. In her view:

> The whole thing is totally mad. Since the gollies were taken and the story was in the newspapers, we have had so many people get in touch with myself and my husband to say we shouldn't give up and should keep them on our shelf. Over the last two days my customers keep singing 'save the gollies' and they want us to get them back. So we are having a sign prepared that will say 'gollies are on display, so don't come in if that offends you' and once that's ready we'll restore some more of the dolls to the shelf.

Essex Police solemnly responded: 'The investigation is ongoing.' And on it went. On 13 April, *The Guardian* reported that the police had been delving into the online messaging of Mrs Ryley's husband Christopher, pub licensee of the White Hart (a name which now sounded slightly sinister). Apropos the hanging dolls, he had made a joke about lynching in Mississippi; he regularly posted on Facebook content from anti-immigrant commentators such as Katie Hopkins. He described Rishi Sunak as 'a Muslim' with arguably xenophobic intent.

He had been photographed in a 'Britain First' T-shirt. His wife Benice defended the picture: 'I don't think Chris is a supporter of Britain First; he was just wearing that shirt because it was convenient at the time.' The police were considering whether his shirt among the other evidence flouted the 1988 Malicious Communications Act.

The investigation continued. The Campaign for Real Ale (Camra) announced that the White Hart would be cancelled from its *Good Beer Guide* 'while these discriminatory dolls continue to be on display'. Substitutes remained behind the bar and six windows at the inn have had bricks thrown through them.* At the time of writing, the White Hart has ceased business under its former management.

MOUTHWASH

In midterm 2021, it was announced that students at Brandeis University in Massachusetts had drawn up a 'suggested language list' and, alongside it, a running website for future suggested usage and non-usage in teaching and social interaction.

Opprobrious language was treated by a tri-categorical listing: (1) term, (2) suggested substitute, (3) explanation. For example: '[*term*] Picnic [*substitute*] outdoor eating [*explanation*] the term picnic can be associated with lynchings of Black people in the United States, during which white spectators were said to have watched while eating.'

---

* For more on golliwogs in literature, see pp. 206–11.

The list was developed, and kept running, by 'students who have been impacted by violence'. Hence everyday terms such as 'take a stab at', 'flogging a dead horse', 'whipped cream' should never ever be used in student social intercourse – whether conversational or electronic. Brandeis is a prestigious school, with a small enrolment (around 5,000), a strong community ethos and a tradition of pastoral care. It was founded in 1948 for Jewish students in the larger Boston area. The institution was historically sensitive to the hurt that abusive language could do.

Brandeis insisted that annihilating words was not, and never had been, what their university was in business for. This etiquette was a student thing. On the other hand, the university had a duty of care. They squirmed and lived with the new verbal conduct rules. They knew they would be royally mocked.

The Brandeis list further mandated that the term 'trigger warning' itself be abolished, on the grounds that it raised anticipatory stress in the vulnerable. It must be replaced by 'content note'. So it was. Four months later, in the UK, the University of Warwick similarly banned the term 'trigger warnings' stating that it will now refer to them as 'content notes', due to the word 'trigger' being deemed too 'provocative' for those on drama and literature courses. Whether picnic lunches and whipped cream were renamed in the Warwick student refectories is not known.

WEAKHEARTS

In August 2022, the *Scottish Daily Express*, inspired by *The Times*' English trigger trawl, surveyed content warnings among Scottish universities. Aberdeen, the paper found, was triggering, among much else, Homer's *Iliad*. The Aberdonian undergraduate was warned that 'killings and woundings are frequent and graphic' in the text. So they are.

For tourists in search of entertainment, the city offers a famous two-hour walk along the 'Bloody Aberdeen Trail'. As advertised: 'The theme of blood splattered granite goes beyond isolated incidents of murder and delves into Aberdeen's rich history of battles, bodysnatching, and official punishments such as drawings, torturing, witch-burning and beheading.'

'Drawing' involves the condemned 'traitor' having their intestines pulled out in front of their dying eyes and burned along with their severed genitals. It is vividly depicted in the last scenes of the film *Braveheart*. Mel Gibson plays William Wallace, the Scottish martyr for the independence of his country from England.

Aberdeen University announced in February 2023 that it would 'decolonise' every course it taught by 2026. Whether that meant, as the Scottish National Party hoped, Scotland would be decolonised by then was up in the air.

GRAVE MATTERS

On 11 June 2020, there were strange doings in the graveyard at St Margaret's churchyard in Rottingdean, East Sussex. Two venerable headstones, already lichen-covered with writing barely visible, were covered with black bin bags and left standing for their imminent removal. The bodies beneath remained to rest in peace.

They belonged to a couple of music hall artists, sixty years buried. The obliteration could be traced back to the BBC's *Today* programme that same June morning, when the edgy comedian Harry Enfield, defending modern blackface routines, had mentioned one of the resting dead at Sussex by their stage name, the 'Chocolate Coloured Coon'.

Within hours of those three inflammatory words being addressed to the nation, the Rottingdean vicar and churchwardens had got busy with the black bags (black was a nice touch, as it happened). The music hall comedian whom Enfield had referred to was George Henry Elliott. At the base of his now blackened headstone was a depiction of drawn theatre curtains and the inscription: 'The last curtain call for G. H. Elliott the Chocolate Coloured Coon who passed peacefully away 19 November 1962. Dearly loved RIP'. The other bin-bagged headstone commemorated 'Alice Banford, Originally known as Lal Cliff, Coon Singer and Dancer, 1884–1962'.

I saw Elliott perform at Regent Music Hall in Ipswich in 1955. His was the headline act. I saw him again, with an audience of 10 million not hundreds, on the TV (black and white) show *This Is Your Life* two years later. There were multiple clips of him in professional chocolate face.

Elliott was an elegant performer. He sauntered on stage. His profile was aquiline; he was not cosmetically thick-lipped like other blackface performers with white greasepaint. There was no cartoon racism in Elliott's demeanour. He was dressed entirely in white to Savile Row standard. He wore a white top hat, a white frock coat, white gloves, cravat, dress shoes and cane.

By skilful use of Leichner greasepaint sticks, Elliott achieved a Dairy Milk chocolate colour. I, like most of the British population, was not affronted by his act in 1955. Like much of the British population in 2023, I would be now. Harry Enfield evidently wouldn't. Born in 1961, he could never have seen Elliott in the flesh.

Elliott had some comic patter – suavely delivered in the faux-toff manner of 'Cardew the Cad' (Cardew Robinson) at a polar music hall extreme from 'cheeky chappies' like Max Miller or 'Little Tich'. Elliott descended in a different genealogical line from Victorian 'Ethiopian Serenaders'. He did not 'jig' or 'tap'. His forte was as a crooner of ballads such as 'Lily of Laguna' (advertised on sheet as 'The World's Greatest Coon Song') or 'Sleepy Time Down South'. Elliott made his real money from 78 rpm records.

Elliott knew America. His family emigrated to the United States when he was four. By the age of nine, he was performing blackface and professionally in a minstrel troupe. The Elliotts returned to Britain in 1901 and George graduated into music hall. He had, unsurprisingly, a convincing mid-Atlantic accent.

Spiked magazine (with pictures of the offending bin bags) was angered by St Margaret's desecration of graves in trust to them. 'Now they're censoring gravestones' was the headline. The church in fact secreted the stones 'in a safe place' and, on 7 December 2023, the vicar and churchwardens successfully petitioned the Consistory Court of the Diocese of Chichester 'to authorise the recutting of the inscription on each headstone such that the offending term is substituted with the expression

"Music Hall Artiste" and to permit the reintroduction of the headstones into the churchyard in the positions they previously occupied'. But not as they previously were.

STORMS AND TEACUPS

On 19 April 2021, the *Daily Telegraph* broke the news that Jane Austen's tea drinking was being 'historically interrogated' as part of Jane Austen's House Museum's current decolonisation of its exhibits – particularly as regards 'slavery links'. The museum is located in the former Austen 'cottage' (in fact a large building) where the author drank tea in the morning (elevenses) and afternoon (teatime) and, one presumes, wrote her fiction between sips.

The *Telegraph*'s story was well sourced. It cited the museum director, Lizzie Dunford, as saying: 'Austen's tea drinking, a key social ceremony in her era and her novels, also links the writer to the exploitation of the British empire.' The Austen family, Dunford pointed out, were purchasers of tea, sugar and cotton and thus 'consumers of the products of the [slave] trade'. Link forged; case closed. The *Daily Express* and *Mail* denounced the 'interrogation' as 'woke madness' and 'Black Lives Matter-inspired'. The story, too delicious not to repeat, went viral.

Teatime with Jane Austen has spawned an industry of china ware and Janeite lore. In the Austens' day, special tea tables, chairs and cabinets as well as crockery and spoons were finely crafted for households which could afford them.

The Austens ordered their tea primarily from Twinings in London. They still could: it thrives. The tassonomics in households like the Austens are, as Dunford suggests, more complex than what the *Telegraph* reported. 'Ceremony' is the appropriate word. Tea itself was during Austen's lifetime a Chinese product. Jane would have drunk loose leaf Chinese black tea ('Bohea'), not pellet-form green tea, nicknamed 'gunpowder' for its excitatory effect. Chinese tea was not the product of systematic British colonial slavery but traded for.

The Chinese monopoly drove prices high, and the government drove them higher – as a middle- and upper-class commodity – by taxation. When Jane was ten years old, in 1784, the Prime Minister, Pitt the Younger, reduced the tea tax from 119 per cent to 12 per cent. Indian ('Assam') tea, rendering it with beer the national English drink, arrived long after her death.

The 'cup that cheers but not inebriates' (the phrase coined by Austen's favourite poet Thomas Cowper) was not sloshed out like *Coronation Street*'s beloved 'brew' but 'served' as ritualistically as communion wine and wafer (biscuits). In houses like the Austens', tea would have been poured not by a servant but by a senior female family member.

The tea set would have been resting on the tea table in preparation. A servant would infuse the tea in the kitchen, traditionally a spoonful for each drinker 'and one more for the pot'. The filled cups would be passed out, one at a time, with polite questioning ('weak or strong?') creating an order of succession, irrespective of rank or gender. Milk, if desired (Chinese tea is better without it), would be put in the cup before the tea. From comments in her letters, it is clear that Jane disapproved of milk or cream. Sugar would be left to the drinker themselves to take according to taste. Jane reportedly had the key to the family sugar cabinet.

Dunford's comment on 'cotton' suggests that from bonnet via unmentionables to the tip of her stocking, Jane Austen's world was moist with slave sweat. During her lifetime and the first wave of the Industrial Revolution, the booming British textile trade imported its raw cotton, along with manufactured cotton goods, from India, via the East India Company, which ran the subcontinent's commerce. The EIC used slave labour and trafficked in slaves during Austen's lifetime.

How much the modern reader wishes to make of such facts and their stains on the nation's beloved books is questionable. But the Austen museum is determined that we should never let them slip our mind when turning the pages.

DOWN WITH SHAKESPEARE!

On 12 December 2016, *Daily Mail* headlines reported with chauvinist alarm that 'students remove Shakespeare portrait at UPenn and replace it with photo of black lesbian writer amid push for diversity at English department'.

UPenn (Pennsylvania University; 'Penn' to its students) is one of the elite eight Ivy League American universities, seven of which were founded during the British possession of the American colonies. Tearing down Shakespeare was, academically, tea chests in Boston Harbor.

Penn students, the *Mail*'s readers learned, had replaced a large reproduction of the Chandos portrait of Shakespeare, which stood a whole wall's length and breadth, at the top of the main staircase in the English literature building, with a large photograph of Audre Lorde. The dismantled portrait of the Bard was delivered by the students to the office of department chair Professor Jed Esty.

Professor Esty took it all in excellent part, telling the *Daily Pennsylvanian* student newspaper that replacing Shakespeare's portrait with that of a black lesbian author was the students' way 'of affirming their commitment to a more inclusive mission for the English department'. Go for it, guys – I'm with you.

Esty was a scholar of recent vintage who had published among much else *A Shrinking Island: Modernism and National Culture in England*. He evidently had no difficulty with Shakespeare shrinking, with his 'sceptred isle' from full wall to dusty storeroom.

Audre Lorde, Harlem born, had devoted her writing life, cut cruelly short by cancer, 'to confronting and addressing injustices of racism, sexism, classism, and homophobia' in prose, fiction, poetry and memoir. One of Lorde's phrases has become the battle cry of the Black Lives Matter movement: 'The master's tools will not dismantle the master's house'.

Penn's 'master' is immortalised by a seven-foot statue dominating the campus. Ben Franklin, then an American Englishman, was the key founder of the university in 1740. Thirty-six years later, as a signatory to the Declaration of Independence, Franklin was one of the founders of modern America, once freed, by war, from English shackles.

His statue, an inescapable presence for Penn's African American students, is not recorded as ever having been vandalised. This sanctity is odd. Franklin owned six household slaves at the period he was instrumental in setting up UPenn. Their names were Peter, his wife Jemima and their sons Othello, George, John and King. Franklin continued owning slaves until 1781, when he was seventy-five years old.

Franklin was – like Thomas Jefferson, who owned 600 slaves during his lifetime – a staunch abolitionist in his later life, when he no longer owned slaves. Like Jefferson (provenly), Franklin is suspected of having sexual relations with at least one of his female slaves.

Jefferson and Franklin (in 1789 a very old, frail man) decided, with others less senior, against including a section in the Constitution against slavery which both ostensibly wished done away with. Time would solve the problem was the thinking of the signatories. Till then, let the master's house stand, along with the UPenn statue of the master. But by 2016, Shakespeare was no longer a welcome guest. 'The hell with that,' Lorde would surely have urged. 'Dump Ben Franklin, you pussies. Is your degree worth that much?'

SAFETYISM

On 4 September 2018, Penguin Books (America) published *The Coddling of the American Mind: How Good Intentions and Bad Ideas Are Setting Up a Generation for Failure* by journalist Greg Lukianoff and psychologist Jonathan Haidt. As described by Moira Weigel in *The Guardian* on 20 September 2018, the authors

> focus on students demanding 'protection' from arguments they find challenging and the professors and administrators who cave in to them. The first section elaborates what the authors call the 'Great Untruths' that supposedly dominate college campuses: What Doesn't Kill You Makes You Weaker; Always Trust Your Feelings; Life Is a Battle Between Good People and Evil People. [The authors'] targets are 'safetyism', the language of microaggressions, identity politics and intersectionality. Generation 'iGen', the one that comes after millennials, is, according to the authors, suffering a mental health crisis because of smartphone addiction and the paranoid parenting style of the upper middle class.

The book made the *New York Times* bestseller list on publication. The neologism 'safetyism' has entered public discourse as a pejorative take on triggering and content warning.

NOT TRIGGERING BUT STABBING

Literature has its outrages perpetrated against authors for being authors. John Dryden, England's first poet laureate, comes to mind being beaten up, to within an inch of his life, by hired 'bullies' ('numerous men unknown') in Rose Alley, off Covent Garden, in 1679 for having been sarcastic about King Charles II and vituperative about the Earl of Rochester in his

'Essay on Satire'. It was probably Rochester who was behind the assault described in the *London Gazette* as 'barbarous'.

One could cite numerous other examples but little, as regards major authors, equals what happened on 12 August 2022. Sir Salman Rushdie, author of *The Satanic Verses* (1989), was about to give a lecture at the Chautauqua Institution, New York, on the US 'as a safe haven for exiled writers'. An ironic title it proved; tragically.

Before speaking to a packed house, Rushdie was approached on stage and stabbed ten times in the face and body. The assailant was Hadi Matar, a 24-year-old first-generation American of Lebanese heritage. His social media profile, police later discovered, revealed pro-Iranian sympathies. He pleaded not guilty when charged in court with second-degree attempted murder on the grounds of religious principle.

The reasons for his act were older than Matar. In 1989, the supreme leader in revolutionary Iran, Ayatollah Khomeini, had delivered a 'fatwa' (irrevocable death sentence) on Rushdie (then a British citizen resident in Britain) for the blasphemies, as perceived, in *The Satanic Verses*. Secular Iranian bodies added a £3 million bounty on Rushdie's head. *The Satanic Verses* revolves around fundamental interpretation of the Quran. Matar admitted to having read the first two pages of the novel, which chronicle a religiously motivated terrorist act. One organisation donated to Matar 1,000 square metres of 'valuable' land for his act.

For several years after its publication (initially under the government of Mrs Thatcher, 'Mrs Torture' in *The Satanic*

Verses), Rushdie was under British state protection. As decades passed, vigilance had lessened: the fatwa, however, could – one was told – never be lifted. Luckily, Rushdie survived Matar's attack. He was grateful to have done so, he gallantly said when he was able to speak publicly again. He had lost the sight of one eye and the use of one hand.

Rushdie had been knighted by the Queen, on Prime Minister Gordon Brown's recommendation, in 2007. Iran threatened revenge for what it conceived as a national insult.

Britain's then current PM, Boris Johnson, was one among many state leaders who were quick to deplore the 2022 atrocity and praise Sir Salman. None, however, could bring themselves to praise *The Satanic Verses*. At the time of writing, Matar has not been convicted.

PUFFINISING

On 18 February 2023, the *Daily Mail* ran the alarmed headline 'Augustus Gloop can't be "fat", the (gender neutral) Oompa-Loompas aren't "small" and even the BFG's gone PC: "Woke" publishing censors REWRITE Roald Dahl's classic books for new editions that remove all language snowflakes might find "offensive"'.

The examples cited were not all that shocking and well short of 'rewriting' or even drastic correction. In *Charlie and the Chocolate Factory*, 'Mrs Salt was a great fat creature with short legs, and she was blowing like a rhinoceros' became 'Mrs Salt was so out of breath, she was blowing like a rhinoceros'. In *The*

Twits, 'Mrs Twit may have been ugly and she may have been beastly, but she was not stupid', became 'Mrs Twit may have been beastly, but she was not stupid'. In *Matilda*, 'Get your mother or father' became 'Get your family'. In *The Enormous Crocodile*, 'We eat little boys and girls' became 'We eat little children'. In *The Fantastic Mr Fox*, 'Bunce, the little pot-bellied dwarf, looked up at Bean' became 'Bunce looked up at Bean'.

As the *Mail* reported, Dahl's publisher, Puffin, the children's arm of Penguin Books, had 'hired sensitivity readers to rewrite chunks of the author's text to make sure the books "can continue to be enjoyed by all today"'. The *Mail* had picked up the story from the *Telegraph* and it was later given lead space by *The Times*. All three papers ran with it and their letters pages seethed.

Puffin had textually harrowed their editions of the books, changed (it seemed) very little and inserted a note on the copyright page of each re-edited and republished title which explained: 'This book was written many years ago, and we regularly review the language to ensure that it can continue to be enjoyed by all.'

Such was the universal protest, led by the grievously assaulted Salman Rushdie, that Puffin gave in. They would, they averred, henceforth bring out two Dahl editions: the 'originals' and the 'revised'. It was strange, given the insignificance of the changes, that the event became a *cause célèbre*. But it touched a sore place which continued to throb. How much were authors' works their own? How much were their readers' lives their own?

JAMES BOND PONDWATERED

After the Dahl imbroglio, another gross case of 'vandalism by woke' was found in the publication of a reissue of the *James Bond* books by Ian Fleming Publications. The series was timed to begin with the seventieth anniversary of the first book in what was now a multi-million-pound franchise, *Casino Royale*.

On 25 February 2023, the *Daily Telegraph* reported that the publishers' hired sensitivity readers had allegedly defanged 007. It was, as with Dahl (see above) and Blyton (see below), slim pickings: only overt uses of the N-word and a few other clumsy racisms were notably altered. *Casino Royale* itself was, one gathered, unviolated.*

Fleming's racist offences crop up more often in his work after, with bestselling success, he retired to Jamaica. In a *Spectator* article of the time (1952), he sighed 'without patience you cannot live and work with coloured people'. He stayed and worked among them, with what patience he could muster, until his premature death.

Of African Americans, Fleming cared to know little other than *Amos 'n' Andy* caricature. His prejudices were freely aired in the depiction of the master-criminal of his second novel, *Live and Let Die* (1954), 'Mr Big' – a West Indian bulk drug supplier to New York's Harlem. Fleming's depiction of African

---

* There were more radical cuts to the released version of the film (2006) in the scene in which Bond's naked testicles are beaten by Le Chiffre with a knotted rope (a carpet beater in the novel). Biographers tell us Fleming was a flagellophile in his personal sexual relations. The English vice.

Americans is given fullest expression in Chapter 5 of the same novel, 'Nigger Heaven' (Heaven being New York's Harlem). The chapter opens:

> At the bus stop at the corner of Fifth and Cathedral Parkway three negroes stood quietly under the light of a street lamp ... 'Yo next, Fatso,' said one of them as the bus came up out of the rain and stopped with a sigh from the great vacuum brakes.
>
> 'Ahm tahd,' said the thick-set man in the mackintosh.

It gets clumsier.

The first description of Mr Big is, by contrast, a white nightmare: 'It was a great football of a head, twice the normal size and very nearly round. The skin was grey-black, taut and shining like the face of a week-old corpse in the river.'

The Ian Fleming Estate, in mitigation of its 2023 edition, pointed out that the author had gone along with required changes to the text of *Live and Let Die* for the American market.

Fleming's own response to those who criticised the brutalities of his work was manly. He was writing, he said, for those who had 'blood not pond water in their veins'. The publishers' defence of their 2023 changes was distinctly pond watery: 'This book was written at a time when terms and attitudes which might be considered offensive by modern readers were commonplace. A number of updates have been made in this edition, while keeping as close as possible to the original text and the period in which it is set.'

Something that 'might be considered offensive by modern readers' is the retained passage in *Casino Royale* where Bond muses, priapically, on imminent intercourse with Vesper Lynd: 'And now he knew that ... the conquest of her body, because of the central privacy in her, would have the sweet tang of rape.'

LITTLE BLACK SAMBO

On 14 October 2019, the Booker Prize panel awarded their annual prize for the year's best novel to both Bernardine Evaristo and Margaret Atwood for *Girl, Woman, Other* and *The Testaments*.

Evaristo was the first woman of African heritage (with Ben Okri she was the second author of Nigerian heritage) to win Britain's – some say the world's – top literary prize for novels in English. It was the Canadian Atwood's second win. Evaristo is an intensely private author and remained so in defiance of the global spotlight thrown on her after October 2019. She keeps herself to herself.

The 'personal life' section of her otherwise lengthy Wikipedia entry is a mere twenty-one words. It is, however, known that she was born (1959) and brought up in Eltham in a large family. She has recorded one salient childhood experience in interview with *The Guardian*:

Our family struggled financially. As my mother didn't return to teaching until her youngest child was of school age, my parents raised eight children on my father's factory salary. Prioritising education, they managed to pay for my oldest brother to attend prep school for a few years. He still recalls the time when his class had to read out loud in turn from the popular racist children's book *The Story of Little Black Sambo* (1899), about Sambo and his father, Black Jumbo, and mother, Black Mumbo. Sambo had long been a racial slur in America and Britain, and mumbo-jumbo was a pejorative term for black languages, which were considered nonsensical. When my seven-year-old brother, the only child of colour in the class, was forced to read from this racist text, everyone in the room erupted with laughter. He has never forgotten it.

Helen Bannerman's *Little Black Sambo* was first published in 1899. It was a first book by a young woman inexperienced in the ways of the British book trade. She sold the copyright for pennies. The tale (no longer hers) went on to make millions for successive publishers well into the 1990s, as Evaristo's above recollection testifies.

'Little Black Sambo' is an Indian boy, pictured in complexion and dress as African. While rambling, decked out in his picturesque garb, the lad meets four tigers who rob him of his clothes and scamper furiously around a palm tree until they melt in a pool of 'ghee', which the hero's mother, Black Mumbo, uses to cook delicious pancakes that night for the family dinner.

Little Black Sambo still sells in the English-speaking and reading world. The latest edition in the UK was in 2010: it received over 1,000 Amazon ratings and an aggregate near max score of 4.5 stars. The reviews record that most of the reviewers (none identifying as, like Evaristo's brother, people of colour) first read *Little Black Sambo* at school. It has always been a hugely popular book in Japan, where it is regarded as not in the slightest racist.

#OWNVOICES

In 2015, as 'trigger warning' was becoming a matter of public debate, youthful Corinne Duyvis published her first novel *Otherbound*. The title is multivalent denoting being 'bound' as with rope (or by disability), along 'with one bound they were free' and 'bound on a journey'. At the same time as her debut novel, Duyvis innovated the genre categorisation of what kind of novel her debut was; namely '#OwnVoices'. She placed that term on her second work, the apocalyptic *On the Edge of Gone* (2016). She insists she does not 'own' the OwnVoices tag, only her 'own' voice within it.

Duyvis is Dutch (which means, ironists will think, she writes better English than some of her English counterparts); she is 'bi' (pronouns she/her) and was diagnosed with autism as a teenager. Her 'disability' (she uses that term) has become another signature Duyvis fiction category. Her repeated assertion is that disability enables a writer.

The imperative of the OwnVoices tag is to give self's voice to those historically 'unselfed' by race, social placement and disability. Duyvis also co-founded the blog 'Disability in Kidlit'. She is young, but her date of birth is withheld.

The second OwnVoices imperative is that author and central character(s) should openly share – generously interpreted – character disability. It does not enforce remaining within your personal disability parameters. Nor is the commonly used term 'young adult' (YA) strictly age restrictive. Inwardness was the essence of OwnVoices, as Duyvis asserted: 'Many people's perceptions – say, of autistic people – are formed by media portrayals created by outsiders. This has far-reaching, damaging consequences. We need to center the people who have historically not been centered, and prioritize their voices in the conversation.'

OwnVoices became within months after its introduction in September 2015 a fluid way of 'web shelving' and a congregational 'talking shop' Twitter conversation. It also created a new genre – YA science fiction with Duyvis's innovative angles. The genre has since become an influential presence in YA books and critical discussion of them.

A co-operative relationship was formed between Duyvis and #WeNeedDiverseBooks (WNDB), a campaigning-for-diversity web initiative founded in 2014 by Asian American writers Ellen Oh and Malinda Lo. The term 'diverse', critical in YA fiction and other writing, presumes 'marginalised' and 'decentred' writing standpoints: these used as creative, not reductive force.

Both OwnVoices and WNDB staked out new, web-borne, generic spaces where different kinds of writing could fertilise among and between themselves and evolve – as, for example, science fiction has over the past 150 years into something that

Jules Verne and H. G. Wells would scarcely recognise but, one fancies, would wonder at.

Duyvis has continued evolving well beyond her initial definitions as a persuasive exponent (in interview mainly) of her beliefs and art.[*]

MOMOCRACY

On 1 January 2021, 'Moms for Liberty' was formed as a non-profit organisation in Florida. Its co-founder, Tiffany Justice, declared herself 'a wife and mom of four school-aged children' and local school board activist. The movement's mission ('innovation'), with local chapters active all over the state, was to assert mothers' rights in schools – specifically books read in class and held in libraries.

The moms' affiliation was avowedly to Governor Ron De-Santis who, for his 2024 presidential campaign, had made school 'brainwashing' of the nation's children (specifically on issues of gender fluidities and critical race theory) a main plank of his vision for America. His press office ensured that official pictures showed him with his wife, 'mom' to his young daughters (something that his arch-rival, Donald Trump, could not do). There was no Stormy Daniels on the DeSantis record. Journalists dug in vain.

'Mom' endorsement became, in short time, influential in elections to school boards. The Moms for Liberty initiative,

---

[*]   For more on Duyvis's *Otherbound*, see pp. 150–53.

using local authority to overthrow the liberal 'orthodoxy' in local schools, was picked up by other states. The result, as PEN America reported, was that 2022 saw a record number of books banned countrywide and any number of teachers anxious about their pay cheques. Moms for Liberty drew up a list of 200 objectionable titles. *Gender Queer*, predictably, headed it.

Schools, dependent on local property tax funding (and teachers likewise for their jobs), were attentive. Moms for Liberty had a particular beef with the novelist Jodi Picoult, who complained in the *Washington Post* that 'Martin County [Florida] is the first to ban twenty of my books at once … a shocking breach of freedom of speech and freedom of information'. Picoult is a permanent presence on the *New York Times* fiction bestseller list. Florida had little time for New York culture nor, apparently, Picoult – an outspoken advocate for freedom of choice on abortion and LGBTQ rights. Florida moms decided she would not speak to their children. The grounds given for banning her was that Picoult's fiction was 'adult romance'. Not for kids generically. It had never, elsewhere, been so classified. Jodi Picoult was no Danielle Steel. Particular exception, in Martin and other Florida counties, was her novel *The Storyteller* 'about the granddaughter of a Holocaust survivor who meets an elderly former SS officer'. 'It has never been banned before,' Picoult told the *Washington Post*.

WHITE KEYS, BLACK KEYS

Following an article in the *Telegraph*, the MailOnline ran a piece on 28 March 2021 entitled 'University of Oxford music faculty considers reforms to address "white hegemony" as staff member raises concerns about music curriculums' "complicity in white supremacy" in light of Black Lives Matter movement'.

Subheads explained what this hegemony in the Dreaming Spires was, namely the 'suggestion to reform music courses to move beyond the classic repertoire. Professor argues curriculum focuses on "white European music from slave period". It is thought that music writing will also be reformed to be more inclusive.'

The article fleshed out the proposed reform to slave period music. Namely, that the department was considering changes to the curriculum, including alternative titles for courses. It was, apparently, staff, or one professor, acting on behalf of students, not students themselves, who were the driving force. The curriculum as reimagined would 'move beyond the classic repertoire, which includes the likes of Beethoven and Mozart, in the wake of the Black Lives Matter movement'.

It was further argued that 'teaching musical notation had not shaken off its connection to its colonial past' and would constitute 'a slap in the face' to some students. European systems of musical notation 'enslaved' colonial African music whose traditions were acoustic not scriptive.

Many of the African American pioneer blues singers in America, creating what is plausibly argued to be one of the greatest art forms to have originated wholly in the USA, could not read or write music. These are deep waters for world musicology.

Documents apparently seen by the *Telegraph* further argued

'that musical skills should no longer be compulsory because the current repertoire's focus on "white European music" causes "students of colour great distress"'. The aim proposed was that composition be reformed 'to be more inclusive' and a 'safe place'. Reportedly, the reforms did not find favour with all those in the faculty. Oxford moves slowly. And sometimes not at all.

NODDY IN THE POISON CABINET

In March 2023, the *Telegraph* reported that in the future at Devon's public libraries any parent, or other adult, requesting a *Famous Five* novel would receive a verbal trigger warning. The volumes were no longer shelved but removed to 'off-limit storage spaces' (i.e. the poison cabinet). Latching on to the *Telegraph*'s breaking story, the *Mail* headlined its page aggressively: 'Uncensored Enid Blyton books with "outdated" language are "being stashed in off-limits spaces by librarians"'. It went on: 'This is to ensure readers don't "stumble upon" some of "outdated language" used'.

Outdated it might be, but doing a Roald Dahl on Blyton had failed twelve years earlier when her publisher, Hodder Childrens' Books, ventured on a wholesale revision. As *The Guardian* then reported: 'Changes made included replacing the word "tinker" with "traveller", "mother and father" with "mum and dad" and "awful swotter" becoming "bookworm". The revisions also made the language more gender-neutral, with the character Anne altered to enjoy teddies instead of dolls.'

In 2016, the publisher withdrew the revised texts; readers didn't like them and weren't buying them.

The 2023 precaution on Blyton was discovered in an FOI Devon County Council investigation. They were, it emerged, no longer directly responsible for their library contents; merely the plant and county council workers servicing it. The lending, reference and technology facilities had been farmed out to a semi-commercial firm, Libraries Unlimited, which 'regularly audits books' and maintains stock acquisition and disposal. Their policy is to keep an eye out for 'outdated' ('unlimited' means what?) language.

Based in Exeter, Libraries Unlimited gives the following description of itself:

Libraries Unlimited believes in enabling everyone to connect to and explore the wider world. We offer welcoming spaces throughout Devon and Torbay which give everyone access to books and a wealth of digital resources, as well as free computer use and WiFi connection. With hundreds of active groups and a year-round calendar of events, we encourage and support everyone to realise their potential and improve their health and wellbeing. By supporting our customers we build communities, enriching lives with ideas, information and inspiration ... We are a company limited by guarantee with charitable status, commissioned by Devon County Council and Torbay Council, and drawing extra support from a variety of funders, partners and collaborators.

The company was registered in 2016 and by 2022 serviced fifty-four 'static' (i.e. building-housed) libraries in Devon and Torbay.

Some things, however, Libraries Unlimited does limit. The *Mail* noted that 'the off-limits area of libraries also contains books that have been removed due to staff or customer complaints – such as the autobiography of previously incarcerated Tommy Robinson, the founder of the far-right English Defence League'.

Poor Enid.

Dr Byrn Harris, legal counsel for the Free Speech Union, told the *Telegraph*: 'We are bemused by the decision to treat the author of *Noddy* as dangerous and subversive samizdat.'

EXIT LARKIN

'"They fuck you up" will clearly be my Lake Isle of Innisfree. I fully expect to hear it recited by a thousand Girl Guides before I die,' Philip Larkin said, in reference to his poem 'This Be The Verse', which begins with the above four words.

England's hand is firmly on the GCSE pantheon of national poets via the OCR (Oxford, Cambridge and RSA) exam boards. Those who are judged 'the truly great'* shifts with the times. Sometimes provocatively. The 23 June 2022 headline on GB News's web-programme minced no words: 'Wilfred Owen,

---

* Stephen Spender's phrase in his most famous poem. He has never made it into the examiners' pantheon.

Philip Larkin and John Keats axed by GCSE exam board for black, disabled and LGBT poets'.

Imagine fifty invisible exclamation marks.

Thomas Hardy and Seamus Heaney were also dropped from the pantheonic forty-five. Fourteen poets of colour were introduced. It could be seen as a sharp cultural reframing. High on the new names were British-Jamaican poet Raymond Antrobus and the Ukrainian-American-Jewish poet Ilya Kaminsky.

Antrobus was in his thirties when canonised for the GCSE syllabus. He speaks to a young, substantially (by age, class and ethnicity) marginalised English constituency. Kaminsky is relevant for other reasons. Not least for the Russian invasion of Ukraine which occurred shortly before the GCSE list was announced. His best-known collection is *Dancing in Odessa*.

His other well-known collection, *Deaf Republic* (like Antrobus, he is hard of hearing), suggests affiliation with the #OwnVoices genre: creativity harvested from within disability and marginality. It's hard to see Kaminsky as English but harder still not to see both poets as writers of current, not traditional, literary interest.

Lieutenant Wilfred Owen's honourable discharge from the OCR list was comprehensible. The Amnesty year 2018 had seen what some saw as orgiastic commemoration of the 'war called great'* and its conclusion. It was, wry observers noted,

---

* The poet Vernon Scannell's phrase. He, like Spender, never made it into the examination pantheon.

a gigantic conflict, but one with grievous damage largely by white males on white males.

Larkin had been a surprisingly long time getting his less honourable discharge from the GCSE syllabus. Since the post-humous publication of volumes of his letters in the 1990s, with the revelation of antediluvian racism, he was deplored by many serious readers. His supporters had had to fight allegations such as those of his fellow poet Tom Paulin that Larkin was the sewer running under the whited sepulchre of British verse.

The additions and deletions to the set poets sorely vexed the then Education Secretary, Nadhim Zahawi, who excoriated it as 'cultural vandalism'. Zahawi's anger was grounded. He had come to England as an Iraqi immigrant, unable (yet) to speak English: 'As a teenager improving my grasp of the English language, Larkin's poems taught me so much about my new home. We must not deny future students the chance to make a similarly powerful connection with a great British author, or miss out on the joy of knowing his work.'

He was, the minister of state said, going to have a word or two with the OCR.

The larger issue, which no one seemed to worry about, was the complete collapse of school readership for classic poetry – Keats, notably, from this year's list.

WHATEVER NEXT?

On 26 March 2023, the *Sunday Mail* picked up the 'vandal-ism by woke' outrage from an article breaking the latest such occurrence in the *Telegraph*. The *Mail* was exasperated beyond measure: 'Now Agatha Christie novels are being re-written! Author's Poirot and Miss Marple mysteries have had original passages reworked or removed by publishers to avoid offending modern audiences. Agatha Christie's novels are the latest works to be rewritten to eliminate verbiage that has been deemed insensitive or inappropriate, it has emerged.'

The story was evidently leaked by a whistleblower on the re-printing publisher's staff, concerned about the textual sanctity of English literature: 'Several of the passages in the author's Poirot and Miss Marple mysteries have reportedly been re-worked or stripped altogether from new editions of the books. Publisher HarperCollins eliminated text containing "insults or references to ethnicity", as well as descriptions of certain characters' physiques.'

'Scores of changes' to her books had been made, it was claimed. Those actually cited were petty. The word 'Oriental', following the influential Edward Said's vilification of the term,* had been removed from *Death on the Nile* (1937), a Poirot mystery. The word 'Nubian', for Egyptian natives, likewise. 'Black' servants no longer 'grinned'. In a Miss Marple tale, *A Caribbean Mystery* (1964), black hotel workers no longer have 'lovely white teeth' or torsos 'of black marble such as a sculptor would have enjoyed'.

As presented, it is, as with Dahl and Fleming, slim pick-ings. Slimmer by magnitudes than Christie's 1939 novel, set

---

* In *Orientalism* (1978).

on 'Nigger Island', initially, and bestsellingly, called *Ten Little Niggers*, then years later retitled *Ten Little Indians* and finally – with successive changes of zeitgeist – *And Then There Were None*. Early reprints, at a period when lynchings of African Americans was still happening in the US, showed a black man hanged by the neck from a tree. Whether Christie was responsible for the changes of title is not clear. But she clearly approved them.

It was clear the Dahl–Fleming–Blyton brouhaha still had life in it. It could still, as Lee Anderson had predicted, steam up the voting public. The *Sunday Mail* article racked up a thousand comments in three hours. Typically furious was the unpunctuated: 'Who are these faceless people let the public know them for what they are bloody idiots or do they come under a taxpayers group of nobodies'.

WOODY ALLEN? TURN HIM OFF

Woody Allen took it very ill when Hachette, having contracted to publish his memoir *Apropos of Nothing* and having paid a hefty advance for it, decided at the last minute (6 March 2020) not to publish the book. For some years, Allen had been in dispute with his ex-partner Mia Farrow and her grown-up children over allegations of intrafamilial sexual molestation.

Allen stood his ground, shifting as it was under his feet:

Cancel culture is the stupidity of our generation. Time will pass, we will look back and it will happen to us as with the

McCarthy era. We will be ashamed of it. And we'll say to ourselves, 'My God, did people really do that and accept it? That teachers be fired, university professors, that scientists be discredited, that actors be put on blacklists?' ... There are already many people who see cancel culture for what it is: an embarrassment.

Hachette's counterstatement betrayed not the slightest embarrassment: 'The decision to cancel Mr Allen's book was a difficult one. At [Hachette] we take our relationships with authors very seriously and do not cancel books lightly. We have published and will continue to publish many challenging books.'

Apropos of Nothing, which they had bought expensively at auction, had evidently overchallenged them. A threatened mass walkout of junior staff had given them no option but to wield the axe.

Cultural indictment of Allen as an alleged criminal who had got away with it was headed by two members of Allen's former family: Dylan Farrow and Ronan Farrow. Both had testified to sexual delinquency by Allen: Dylan recorded it as having been directed at herself.* Ronan was one of the movers of what formed itself into the #MeToo protest movement and was himself an Hachette author.

Since a third of Allen's book controverts his son's campaign against him (including aspersions on Ronan's being not his but Frank Sinatra's son), it is astonishing that Hachette needed

---

* Two police investigations found no charges to bring against Allen.

a threatened staff walkout to persuade them that the two authors could never rest peacefully alongside each other on their backlist.

The cancellation of Allen was controversial in the book world. 'The Hachette decision to drop the Woody Allen book makes me very uneasy,' said Stephen King on Twitter. 'It's not him; I don't give a damn about Mr Allen. It's who gets muzzled next that worries me.' Allen walked away with all rights and his advance. The book was picked up by Arcade Publishing. It made number fifteen on the *New York Times* non-fiction bestseller list on publication.

HARRY POTTER BURNS

On 2 February 2022, in Nashville, Tennessee, the pastor Greg Locke led an outdoor service of conflagration burning copies of J. K. Rowling's *Harry Potter* books. He told his congregation that when lighting the fire: 'We will be in our continued series of acts on Deliverance from Demons. We have stuff coming in from all over that we will be burning. We're not playing games. Witchcraft and accursed things must go.'

The Revd Locke is a Trump supporter. His bonfire, one of many such Potter exorcisms, is posted on YouTube.

On another front, in September 2020, *Newsweek* reported a spate of Potter burnings in protest against Rowling's views on gender. In addition to being the most popular of all time child-print novel series, Rowling's Potteriad is the most publicly put to the torch.

StoryGraph has twenty-seven 'graphic' content warnings. Demonism is not listed. 'Genocide' is.

THE HANDMAID'S NOT FOR BURNING

As it had every year since its runaway success as a TV series in 2017, Margaret Atwood's *The Handmaid's Tale* had consistently been among the top-ten most-banned books in the US (by CBS annual count) in 2021.

Across the Atlantic, at Manchester University, the 1985 book (which first conquered a male-dominated world as a prize-winning work of science fiction, not feminist protest) was menacingly triggered in an undergraduate course on modern fiction. Students were told: 'Content Warning: This week's novel [*The Handmaid's Tale*] contains disturbing passages (rape, violence, and suicide).' A 2019 regulation at Manchester allowed any student to walk out of a class they felt threatened by.

Atwood has a wry sense of humour. She appeared, smilingly, in a spiritual cameo, as a kind of vision of Margaret, in the first TV series. She likes to remind US readers that she blows their way from Canada – where the bad weather comes from. And in June 2022, she presented PEN America with a specially designed 'unburnable' copy of *The Handmaid's Tale* to support the society's fight against censorship. The asbestoid volume sold at Sotheby's for $130,000. The 82-year-old author got herself a trigger-operated flamethrower and posted a picture of herself on YouTube blasting the book. The book survived.

So has Atwood. So, with its umpteenth TV series, does *The Handmaid's Tale*.

'PROBLEMATIC' FOR STUDENTS

In 2005, Columbia University offered an optional course entitled 'CLEN 4521: Topics in Comparative Literature: The World of Banned Books'. The instructor was Professor Jonathan E. Abel. His research interest was 'censorship as an apparatus of the state'. The course was restricted to English majors to exclude any undergraduate from other places curious about dirty books. The course was oversubscribed.

In the eleventh week of Professor Abel's semester-long course, the text under consideration was Vladimir Nabokov's *Lolita*. *Reading Lolita in Tehran* (2003) by Azar Nafisi (Nabokov's novel is banned in Iran) was recommended as secondary reading. Historically, in the late 1950s, *Lolita* was originally as unpublishable in America as Tehran. 'Do you think I'm crazy?' one American publisher asked Nabokov. *Lolita* was first published in Paris, in 1955, by Maurice Girodias's Olympia Press. Girodias proudly proclaimed himself the niche publisher of the English 'db' (dirty book).

Nabokov's book, once liberated in the English-speaking world, was applauded. The plot – fifty-year-old man, violating his eleven-year-old stepdaughter for months on end – was vindicated by linguistic style: or so it was claimed. Over time, the two films of *Lolita* (in one of which she looks older than him) treated the subject awkwardly. What was worse was that the title became the catchword for the vilest pornography.

The climate had changed. Fifteen years after CLEN 4521 was advertised in their *Catalog*, Columbia, under pressure from English majors, desyllabused *Lolita* from all courses at the university. The reason given was that the novel could be 'problematic for students'.

PART TWO

MACHINERIES

THE MACHINES IN JANE AUSTEN'S GARDEN

The website Trigger Warning Database (hereafter TWD), founded in 2021, lists searchable alerts on 6,000 or more books supplied by voluntary contributors. Jane Austen's works, to take one example, contain the following caveats: 'anti-ziganism [racism towards Romani people]' (*Emma*), 'incest' (*Mansfield Park*), 'classism' (*Pride and Prejudice*) and 'animal hunting (mentioned)' (*Sense and Sensibility*).

These triggers, like the database's others, are categorical across the sample, not one-book characteristics. A general search by keyword will, for example, throw up many racism alerts – from Mark Twain (occasional) to Stephen King (persistent offender) to Neil Gaiman (likewise) to J. K. Rowling (few but intense) and Shakespeare. This is not company one would automatically expect Jane Austen to keep.*

---

*   In an incidental scene Harriet, Emma's protégée, is alarmed by meeting a band of gypsies who do her no harm.

TWD is not to be confused with the website Book Trigger Warnings (hereafter BTW). It has much the same warnings on Austen but adds 'age gaps (period typical)' (*Sense and Sensibility*), 'implied grooming/predatory behaviour' (*Emma*) and 'neglect' (*Mansfield Park*). In this database, one detects a rather more sinister hand under the glove.

BTW, unlike TWD, invites visitable essay-length opinion ('build your page') on the book in question by contributors. Opinionation was taken a step further by Goodreads. The site was conceived, small-time, in 2007 by Elizabeth Khuri Chandler, who had a passion for Jane Austen, particularly *Pride and Prejudice*. Elizabeth Bennet, she says, helped the young Elizabeth Khuri define herself as a woman.

She was inspired by her Austenphilia to found an internet reading group with the aid of her web-designer husband Otis. They trademarked it 'Goodreads'. Registration was required for write-in contributors but not for looky-loo visitors. Books were graded by writers on a one-to-five-star scale. Reasons (including numerous 'soft' triggerings in the form of specified 'dislikes') were welcome at up to short essay length. The longer ones were abbreviated with the option ('more') of continuing or stopping ('less') when enough had been read. The more/less option worked as a spoiler alert mechanism.

Goodreads crested the blogging wave of the early twenty-first century and within months boasted half a million registered, write-in, members. It was the largest 'readers' group' in the world. It organised 'readers' as a critical force stronger, by virtue of common reader mass, than newspaper, magazine and academic know-alls. Goodreads was 'the people'.

The book trade smelled money, particularly with the explosively growing number of look-in visitors. Goodreads was an internet shop window and endorsement machine. And unlike advertising, it cost nothing and needed no staff to keep it going. It was self-propelled. Goodreads' hook was that its criticisms and comments were 'felt' and from all kinds and classes of readers with only two things in common. They loved books. They bought books.

Consequently, in 2013, Amazon bought Goodreads, now swollen to 20 million members, for a cool $150 million (thank you, Jane Austen). It now serves as a latch-on to Jeff Bezos's massive online sale catalogue.* ARCs ('advanced reading copies') were supplied, one can be sure, to relied-on 'influencers'. The original format was nonetheless retained.

Goodreads remains cost-free to visitors but carries ads. By 2019, Amazon–Goodreads had 90 million members. It boasted itself the web's largest 'social book cataloguing website'. Soft triggering and hard endorsement remained the core part of its make-up.

By 2020, the World Wide Web was an open sesame for the student, the researcher, the schoolteacher, the professor and the purchaser-booklover. Everything from the Domesday Book to this summer's beach book was accessible online. For

---

* The 'reviews' the catalogue contains are often, unlike Goodreads verdicts, regarded as dubious.

students, tracking down, say Jane Austen, this access could be drawn on in collaboration with SparkNotes. This free site was a descriptive-annotation literary text resource, initially called 'Spark', started as a co-operative venture by four English studies cream of the cream Harvard students in 1999. Spark-Notes did not trigger but was critical: often sharply so. The mega-publishing house Barnes & Noble bought it in 2001 for $3.5 million. All college students, lumbered with vast tuition debt, should have been so lucky as the SparkNotes four.

Gutenberg, the free e-library devised by one of the heroes of modern goodreading, Michael S. Hart, in 1971, was, fifty years later, 70,000 out-of-copyright volumes strong. Hart, alas, was no longer alive to see his work. Along with the free Wikipedia (many of whose anonymous literary entries are, despite academic sneers, first rate), Hart's ethereal library has enlarged and deepened the environment in which literature, past and present, is rooted and lives. For students at the postgraduate level and scholars, there is JSTOR, the electronic archive of learned journals. Institutional membership makes it free for most users.

For mere book lovers, the old *Wunderkammer* of the second-hand bookshop, smelling so wonderfully of tired old, former owner-inscribed volumes, and long-gone page-turning licked index fingers, has been replaced by e-facilities such as AbeBooks (Advanced Book Exchange). Preowned volumes are available, rush order, with next-day delivery, often at near-giveaway price, plus P&P.

The web has created a constellation of scholarly and casual

reader resources, but pessimists might wonder where all these easy roads were leading to. And at what junction they would combine to create the 'singularity' – that point, forecast by the *Terminator* film franchise, when all machineries become one. Skynet for books.

The online machinery was, for thorough-going users, already an apparatus which took away a sizeable chunk of the work of aimless browsing, reading and thinking for you. But did you, as a reader, really want to part with doing it all yourself? There were, one might fear, too many short cuts and too much down-loadable material. At what point did reading become injection? On social media and blogs, there was an army of 'reading influencers' with their seductive faux intimacies. The scholar adventurer might feel themselves in danger of becoming a kind of cyborg. Or cog. What would the Great God in the Cloud, AI (artificial intelligence) do when it had this array of machinery in its dictatorial power? The whole shebang was, according to Moore's Law, doubling its efficiency every year.

With such questions, particularly 'influencing', in mind, one of the most thought-provoking innovations of the 2020s is the website StoryGraph. It is a facility devised and founded in 2019 by the software engineer Nadia Odunayo, a graduate of Oxford. Like pre-Amazon Goodreads, StoryGraph targeted book lovers; like Odunayo herself, evidently. It fostered 'buddy reading' and 'personalised recommendation' – the 'book for you'. Just you. As the founder puts it: 'I thought, "What if I could build a website that could be like your trusted friend, but it knew about all sorts of books?"'

As StoryGraph's latest (2023) sales pitch promises, it's an exclusively 'all for you' thing: 'We'll help you track your reading and choose your next book based on your mood and your favorite topics and themes.'

Its tracking/choosing operation is planets ahead of the 'like/dislike' subjective clicks of Instagram or other social media sites, or Goodreads' subjective star ratings.

Odunayo was young when she devised StoryGraph and part of her inspiration and modelling was based on the phenomenally successful dating and marriage-broker websites, such as eHarmony. StoryGraph will profile you, the book reader, from patterns of consultation and consumption and self-definitional tags – then 'marry' you with the right book.

StoryGraph anatomises books categorically, with analysis and summary of 'community belongingness', 'tropes', 'mood' and whether a text is 'plot- or character-driven'. It will locate 'matches' and, by sequential techno-analysis of book and personal data, the glass slipper will slide onto your foot.

StoryGraph invites living authorial consent to comment on its categorisation. Some writers accept the offer. As it has evolved over its brief lifetime, StoryGraph is 'freemium'. A large chunk is free: premium stuff must be paid for. In 2021, StoryGraph began to introduce content warnings – triggering – both soft and hard.

So what, to Austenise once more, does StoryGraph make of *Pride and Prejudice*?

On 'moods' and tone, Austen's novel is 'lighthearted' according to 72 per cent of readers, with 57 per cent finding it 'funny',

49 per cent 'emotional', 31 per cent 'hopeful', 31 per cent 're-laxing' and 25 per cent 'reflective'. There follows a slump, with only 14 per cent of readers thinking it is 'inspiring', 9 per cent 'challenging', 7 per cent 'adventurous', 3 per cent 'tense', 2 per cent 'informative', 1 per cent 'mysterious' and 1 per cent 'sad'.

As regards 'pace', 52 per cent of readers found it 'slow', 42 per cent 'medium' and 4 per cent 'fast'. Is it plot- or character-driven? A majority of 64 per cent voted for 'character', with 28 per cent saying it was 'a mix' and 6 per cent thinking 'plot'.

Strong character development? Yes, say 91 per cent of readers. Loveable characters? Yes, according to 84 per cent. Diverse cast of characters? No, conclude 80 per cent. Flaws of characters a main focus? Yes, deem 85 per cent. The book's average rating (out of five) is a high 4.31.

This breakdown of the doings at Longbourn comes entirely from StoryGraph users. The book itself will, where 'matches' are found, be recommended to other members fitting their personal profiles. Publishers follow StoryGraph avidly. They see booktopia in it – programmable purchasers: Dr Johnson's 'common reader' (with whom he loved to concur) metamor-phosed into reading's Strasbourg goose.*

DOES THE DOG DIE?

The English, as Vladimir Nabokov contemptuously noted, re-serve their pity for the blind man's dog. Does the Dog Die? is

---

* Luckless birds who have over-rich food funnelled down their throat until their livers burst creating the delicacy *foie de gras*.

a warning website flagging 'crowdsourced emotional spoilers for movies, TV, books and more'. It currently has 160 flagged response categories.

The site was founded in 2010 with just the one topic – signalled in the title – by John Whipple, a software developer. As John recalls: 'It was originally my sister's idea. She found it frustrating to watch a movie with a dog in it because worrying over the survival of the dog made it impossible to enjoy the movie.'

Both Whipples were dog lovers. John had lost his long-term four-legged friend some years earlier and found, he said, 'doglessness so intolerable that he adopted a puppy within twenty-four hours'.

Neither, however, were dog soppy. Whipple's sister had read Blake Snyder's hilariously cynical screenwriting manual *Save the Cat!* (2005) which confirmed her sense that media is not served up merely to entertain: it has furtive designs on you. In his book, Snyder lays down a number of rules for successfully pitching the script which will become a successful movie. The first is that in an early scene the hero should do some superfluous 'good' act that has nothing to do with the main plot. What Snyder alluded to was the first movie (1978) of the *Superman* series, where the Man of Steel, before saving the world from Lex Luthor, rescues a cat from up a tree.

It was the viewer manipulation as much as any actual assault on the sensibility (chain-saw massacre style) that Whipples, brother and sister, began by focusing on and triggering against. Another film, *The War of the Roses* (1989), serves as illustration. The Roses, a married couple, embark on a darkly comic embattled divorce. The wife, a chef, as a pseudo peace gesture, prepares a canapé with a delicious *pâté* for her husband which he eats with relish; only to be told he's been eating his beloved pooch Benny ('Good to the last bite,' his wife sneers). The Thyestean scene is graphically there in the source novel, but the film loses its nerve and shows a passing glimpse, at the end of the film, of Benny in the bushes outside.* Both Roses have died in a mutual homicide.

So the dog dies in one narrative; and the dog survives in another narrative. Would it spoil the film for you if it really was Benny on the biscuit not the bushes? Some would say yes. Others, like the Whipples, might find it a touch too Buñuel.

For some months, Does the Dog Die (hereafter DDD) focused on canines in film and TV (occasionally sourcing books). Whipple and his sister were joined by a corps of dog-loving friends. The name was trademarked. It eventually took off with a crowdsourcing interface, again designed by John.

DDD went on to become more than pet-centric. Users proposed their personal triggerable categories about things, other than dog survival, which had 'ruined it' for them and that others ought to be warned about. If there were a sufficient number of contributors of the same mind, the ruinous element would evolve into a categorical trigger. Or a reassurance. Whipple cites the 'wisdom of crowds', *E pluribus unum*, as validation of the website's procedure.

---

* The novel, 1981, is by Warren Adler.

Does the Dog Die has, via its crowdsourcing, gone far beyond its initial canine mortality/immortality category. 'Cannibalism' (one species up from Benny) currently rates highly triggerable with the popularity of the *Living Dead* TV genre and its many knock-offs. There was, Whipple records, a suggested category for 'Does the Dragon Die'. It didn't make it.

Some triggers less obviously crowdsourced are listed as worrisome categories. For example: 'misophonia'. The word may not be in every TV watcher's or cinema-goer's vocabulary. Does the Dog Die explains:

> Misophonia, or 'selective sound sensitivity syndrome', is a neurological disorder often associated with autism and ADHD, in which hearing mouth noises or repetitive sounds like eating, chewing gum, smacking lips, tapping, and other noises when eating, triggers anger, disgust, or even physical pain. Many movies and TV shows have moments like this, with some that are so extreme it becomes unwatchable for viewers who suffer from this.

For the 2020 film adaptation of Jane Austen's *Emma*, there are the following four misophonic 'trigger' response records: 'Harriet [the hero's protégée] makes sounds while nibbling pasties at tea.' There are, as well, for this film sixteen 'yes' votes for 'does an animal die (besides a dog, cat or horse)?' category, noting that 'a dead goose is shown'. I, personally, can't recall if it's eaten.

Chris Norris is an American journalist and dog lover. He

is dog-loving enough to have created, in memory of his deceased 'Westie' terrier Gus, a caninophile website, 'The Wildest'. Norris has given the Whipples and DDD much thought. He recalls:

> Movies often tell us what stage of life we're in – how our priorities may have shifted, what we can no longer tolerate onscreen. My doctor sister – a karate blackbelt unafraid to intubate someone or deliver their baby – found, after having her first kid, that she could not watch *Finding Nemo*, a G-rated Pixar adventure full of wholesome life lessons, which begins with the wholesale slaughter of a mom and nearly all of her children. She realized that kind of fare was off her menu.

Norris highlights John Whipple's point about realising two things: '1) many of the things we track aren't a big deal for most people, and 2) every human on this earth has at least one thing that is a big deal [to them] if they're surprised by it in a movie.'

Norris proposed a 'community question' with a yes/no answer request: 'Would you skip a movie because the dog dies?' It has elicited, at time of writing, 1,800 responses. They break down as: 'Yes – *That's a dealbreaker!* 48 per cent' and 'Nope – *I can handle it.* 52 per cent'.

More complex, perhaps, would be the question 'Would you skip an animal-centric film in the making of which you are told an animal was killed?' The opening titles of Alfred

Hitchcock's *The Birds* reassure us that none of the feathered tribe were killed. As was no actual goldfish, we are assured, in *A Fish Called Wanda*. Forty-eight piglets were employed in *Babe*; all, we are assured, were disposed of alive in comfortable styes to live out their moments of stardom before taking the one-way journey to pork chops.

For American-produced films, only the American Humane Association can warrant the statement 'No Animals Were Harmed in the Making of this Movie' on the titles or credits of a film. It has registered 'unacceptable' on such things as the actual hacking to death of a water buffalo with machetes at the climax of *Apocalypse Now* (1979). That judgement does not accompany the film onscreen. Morally, it should. But what if you were warned *before* you saw it?

Does the Dog Die is based on observed human psychology and takes triggering well beyond any pooh-poohing accusations of snowflakery or weak knees and into very interesting places. As Ben Lindbergh notes, on his 'Ringer' pop culture website, three social science professors at Colorado University ran an experiment and published a paper entitled 'Are People More Disturbed By Dog or Human Suffering?'

Some 250 undergraduates were 'asked to indicate their degree of empathy for a brutally beaten human adult or child versus an adult dog or puppy, as described in a fictitious news report'.

The results suggested that humans experience more empathy for fictitious human children, puppies and adult dogs than for fictitious adult humans. One of the authors, Professor

Leslie Irvine, explained: 'Dogs boast elite-level neoteny, or the retention of juvenile characteristics into adulthood. Those juvenile characteristics stimulate caregiving behavior in humans, an evolutionary response that encourages adults to take care of their young.'

Take that, Vladimir.

WHITHER THE BOOKWORLD?

On New Year's Day 2022, James Frey was named CEO of Andbox, a New York-based esports organisation. It seems like the kind of fact which would be at home in the financial pages of the *New York Times*. But the niggling question is: what is 'esports'?

It's a relevant question because Frey encapsulates the 21st-century evolution of the book world into worlds outside of its traditional selfhoods. He is, by nature, an opportunist with an uncannily keen eye as to where and what the next new thing will be. New things are, currently, coming thick and fast.

James Frey first made headlines with his memoir – a drunkalog – in 2003. It was called *A Million Little Pieces*. So-called 'misery memoirs' (Rousseauistic confessions) were en vogue: propelled by the rise of twelve-step groups where those in recovery would spill out their all to fellow sufferers.*

Frey's drunkenness was, as he recounted it, high order misery. But he'd put his little pieces back together. He was one

---

* Mine, *Last Drink to LA*, was published in 2001, revised in 2015.

of the recovering.* The book was picked up by Oprah and, after a tell-all interview, it was put on the Great Influencer's book recommendation list. Frey was a 'made man'. Until, that is, the website Smoking Gun did some digging and found his account was, in large part, made up. Despite its proven balder-dash, the book continued to sell but moved over to the *New York Times* fiction bestseller list.

There was a barrage of complaints from Frey's fooled readers, which resulted in a class-action lawsuit under trade description acts that cost Frey's publisher $2.35 million. He outlived his pariahdom, after more confessions, and wrote some more fiction – but nothing as big as his debut venture. Some admired him for having gamed the 'industry'. And, for James Frey, industry, not art, was what it was.

In 2010, he saw the glint of gold in YA fantasy (he was now forty years old). For a year or so, he gave talks to creative writing students in universities around New York – usually on 'emotional' truth trumping fact. Lies were the higher truth. Creative writing was a growth area with a multitude of wan-nabes desperate to get their foot in the door. Most would have their toes bruised and limp off to find some other way of put-ting bread on their table. Tuition cost up to $50,000 a year.

Frey gave himself an authorial pseudonym, Pittacus Lore, and set up Full Fathom Five, otherwise known as 'James Frey's Fiction Factory'. Andy Warhol's Factory, he said, 'is an example of that way of working'. He was similarly impressed by Damien

---

* I reviewed it favourably. My encomium was plastered on the UK paperback cover before Frey was unmasked.

Hirst's art factory (how many people did Damien have working for him, 120?). 'That's what I'm doing with literature,' Frey brazenly admitted. It was one up from *Nineteen Eighty-Four*'s 'pornosec', where pornography is machine produced.

Creative writing recruits were routinely given $250 for narratives 'polished' by Pittacus Lore, alias James Frey or other scriptists. In YA fiction, particularly YA sci-fi and fantasy, it was the 'gimmick' (what dinosaur Hitchcock called the 'McGuffin'), not the words, which were the story's mainspring. And there's no copyright in gimmicks.

The Frey Factory developed the *Lorien Legacies* series, hoping it would be the next *Twilight* or *Hunger Games*.* The first volume was entitled *I Am Number Four*. The former Columbia creative writing student Jobie Hughes was Frey-Lore's silent partner. He wrote four drafts. Frey 'improved' them. He was the man.

The basic plot centres on nine 'Loric' aliens who were chased from their home planet by evil 'Mogadorians'. The Loricians now live on earth 'in the guise of teenagers'. An alien war is raging on earth invisible to the earthling masses – teenagers, however, are tuned in. Half a dozen instalments of the saga were in prospect.

Frey is a salesman of genius. He contrived to interest Steven Spielberg. Million-dollar options were in play.

The kick-off novel (by 'Pittacus Lore') had come out in 2010:

---

* For further details on these matters, see Suzanne Mozes, 'James Frey's Fiction Factory', *New York Magazine* (11 November 2010); and Will Leitch, 'Backstory: James Frey's Idea Factory and *I Am Number Four*', *Yahoo! Entertainment* (17 February 2011).

'packaged' by Full Fathom Five and published by Harper-Collins. It shot to number one on the *New York Times* children's bestseller list and stayed in it for weeks.

The film came out in 2011. With DVD added, the multiform *I Am Number Four* generated good money and bad reviews. It was not, it transpired, the new *Hunger Games*. The spark was missing. The Rotten Tomatoes influencer website gave it 33 per cent on the 'Tomatometer' and, as 'critics' consensus', the site's verdict was: 'It's positioned as the start of a franchise, but *I Am Number Four*'s familiar plot and unconvincing performances add up to one noisy, derivative, and ultimately forgettable sci-fi thriller.'

Jobie Hughes left, as unknown by authorial name as when he had arrived. Other destined unknowns took his place as inspirers. Full Fathom Five saw the *Lorien Legacies* through to its drooping end. But the company was moving up and on, as its ads proclaimed, with 'its most ambitious project to date: a multi-platform series called *Endgame* that will feature a geo-location game (created by Google), a series of books and novellas co-written by Frey (to be published by Harper-Collins), and a forthcoming film adaptation (being produced by 20th Century Fox).'

Endgame would be interactive on various media outlets and delivery systems. Frey realised that if the book market was to catch up with technology, it must do so via young users, not old readers who really wanted public libraries, main street booksellers and Oprah's reading club. The future was digitation, the iPhone and tablet, not print and page – even if Kindled.

Endgame reportedly pulled in million-dollar advances. Three 'stages' were scheduled over as many years. It would 'collide' book, film, keyboard, 'novella' (electronic or print). As Frey explained to *Publishers Weekly*:

> It was conceived as a project that would exist across multiple platforms, and that the story would be told in books, novellas, games, film, and TV. [We also knew it] would have a social media presence, and exist in places – such as search results and mapping coordinates and YouTube – that aren't traditionally mediums for storytelling and writing.

He gave out the plot. It had a Genesis feel to it (although a declared atheist, Frey was, in his later years, increasingly preoccupied with Christianity). There is a strong whiff of '*Left Behind*' and 'rapture' apocalypticism in the enterprise, as described:

> Long ago, an alien race known as 'Makers' descended upon earth and gave civilization to humans in exchange for gold. When they left, they promised to return some day and when they do, a game will initiate that will determine the fate of mankind, the titular Endgame. Ever since, the twelve original lines of mankind have been preparing for this event. Each line always has a player available, an adolescent between the ages of 13 and 19. Players are trained in all sorts of skills, combat and survival tactics to ensure their line's victory should Endgame ever start at some point.

The story begins when twelve meteor strikes on seemingly random places of earth signal the start of Endgame. The players gather at the starting point of Endgame and the race for the fate of man begins.

Everything this phenomenal ideas-merchant does is a prelude to the next thing he will do. Hence the announcement in the trade papers in January 2022: 'Author James Frey Writing New Career Chapter As CEO Of NY Esports Organization Andbox'. Andbox, which rebranded to NYXL shortly after Frey's ascent, owns and operates the New York Excelsior, the city's first professional esports team (if you're somewhat lost, it will be helpful to look up the informative Wikipedia entry on esports).

Excelsior competes in Call of Duty and Overwatch Leagues. As Andbox described itself:

As the hub for New York's gamers, we're transforming the way people experience and express their love for gaming through exclusive content, behind the scenes looks into the world of esports, and unique stories and perspectives from every corner of gaming.

Andbox is an esports organization that embraces the relentless energy of competitive gaming and New York City alike. Through fielding professional teams like Overwatch League's NYXL, creating desirable apparel collections with renowned designers, and hosting experiences throughout the city, Andbox's mission is to be a cultural conduit that fuels and elevates all aspects of the gaming world.

Our goal in naming the organization was to create something that could act as a platform for their range of unique offerings as well as feel at home in NYC and the gaming community. The name Andbox is derived from the term 'sandbox', which in gaming refers to an open-world environment that allows players to roam freely and explore. The identity itself plays off the same core idea, a canvas for a new kind of creativity, one that is constantly evolving, adapting and growing. The design system draws equal inspiration from gaming as it does NYC, based on a square grid, modular yet highly energetic. The graphic language is a vibrant celebration of convergence, by colliding gaming, culture and creativity.

Good luck with that.

James Frey is a multiple success story and a multiple crash and burn story, a succession of 'collisions' banging his way through his region of the literary world and its ever more unbookish mutations like a pinball.

He is, I fear, a portent of the shape of things to come. At warp speed and effect.

ALL THE 'ITIES'

Not, as one might fantasise, a hitherto unknown work by Roald Dahl, up there with *The Twits*, but a lexicon of doubleplusgood words (to borrow Orwell's Newspeak) in current debates about children's literature – books for the formative mind. The 'ities' are 'sensitivity', 'inclusivity', 'diversity', 'universality', 'authenticity' and, as regards 'disability', body 'positivity'.

A commercial name which recurs often in cases of the moral revision of literary texts, particularly those aimed at children, is Inclusive Minds (hereafter IM). Among other consultative services, IM supplies 'readers', equipped with fingertip sensitivity, to help achieve the collectivity enshrined in its name and its mission to spread inclusivity. As it defines itself:

> Founded in January 2013, Inclusive Minds is an organisation that works with the children's book world to support them in authentic representation, primarily by connecting those in the industry with those who have lived experience of any or multiple facets of diversity.
>
> When Inclusive Minds launched over 10 years ago, it played a valuable role in helping to raise awareness of the importance of better and more authentic inclusion in children's books. The organisation has always evolved with the changing needs of the industry and as awareness of the need for diversity and inclusion has dramatically risen in recent years there is less need for Inclusive Minds to campaign for books to be inclusive, and a greater need for the practical services we offer in terms of helping ensure authenticity.

To help achieve this are their 'inclusion ambassadors': 'This is a network of young people with many different lived experiences who are willing to share their insight to help them in the process of creating authentically – and often incidentally – inclusive books. They are not sensitivity readers.'

Some of their 'inclusion ambassadors', the *Daily Mail* noted, in shock, were 'eight years old'. Out of the mouths of babes and sucklings… or perhaps just babble.

IM had begun in 2013 as a 'collective' of similarly minded YA women. Such is capitalism that it aged out and 'in February 2020 Inclusive Minds became a Community Interest Company (CIC) with a team of Ambassadors with lived experience as directors'. It bought in but didn't sell out or forget its initial impulse.

One of IM's co-founders, Alexandra Strick, is 'an author who is keen to see everyone represented in books and all children having a real voice'. Her professional autobiography records her progress through voluntary work with children at university to postgraduate service with children's charities. Her interest was, consistently, in literate children below the age of ten. Child protection was another interest: 'With Lottery funding (and based at a national disability charity Whizz-Kidz), she worked with many young disabled people across the UK, helping them to set up and deliver projects which would improve access and inclusion and challenge attitudes.'

On the side, Strickland co-wrote the picture book *Max the Champion*, which 'aimed to include aspects of disability never before featured in books, subtly and positively. It contains over forty tiny visual references to disability, without any mention in the text'. As an enthusiastic review on the Little Parachutes website describes it:

Sport-mad Max turns aspects of his daily routine into day-dreams of major sporting events. As he dives into his cereal, he imagines plunging into an Olympic-sized swimming pool (and receiving a perfect score of ten). With a sprinkle of fantasy, his bike ride to school is transformed into a high-speed bobsleigh descent. The story is packed full of visual references to disability and inclusion: children in wheelchairs, oxygen tubes, leg braces and eye patches can be spotted in the illustrations, as can a child with cherubism. Max himself wears a hearing aid and uses an asthma inhaler.

As things are at the moment, Inclusive Minds, or operations like it, seem destined to go from strength to strength. It is hard not to approve of its doing so, although it is as easy to resent its hectoring, rigid core, self-righteousness about not what children like but what they should like.

THE LAW

For about the first seventeen years of my reading life (I deduct the initial preliterate five), I was under a protective legal shield that, until puberty, I was largely unaware of and, after puberty, I bitterly resented and, once adult in a cautious way, I went on to defy.

I read the Parisian DB (dirty book) version of D. H. Lawrence's *Lady Chatterley's Lover*, by the Seine, in 1954 aged sixteen. But I did not dare bring the volume back through

UK customs. Not that I was all that impressed by the novel. I recall thinking, in a condition of total erectionlessness, that all that guff about thrilled loins and shapely haunches was too vague and wordy compared to *White Thighs* by 'Frances Lengel' (a woman!), which I bought at the same time. (In fact, *White Thighs* was written, for money, with a lot of other 'filth' titles, by the experimental young novelist Alexander Trocchi, making ends meet so he could get on with his real fiction.) *White Thighs* went with *Lady Chatterley* for a swim in the Seine after I'd done with them.

Times change. *White Thighs* is now available for £9.45 on Amazon and, as one reviewer on Goodreads describes it (two stars): 'Spoilers included. Look, I've read a lot of erotica, but this one is pretty off the charts as far as surprises go. It starts out a normal-ish English influenced crops and caning and nanny and a bit of D/s but evolves into branding, harem, M/s, necrophilia, and snuff.'*

The unwanted shield between sixteen-year-old John Sutherland and his books was the 1857 Obscenity Publications Act. It had one main criterion for obscenity (called the 'Hicklin test'). Books with a 'tendency to deprave and corrupt those whose minds are open to such immoral influences, and into whose hands a publication of this sort may fall' were criminal. It was so loosely defined, cynics noted, that the New Testament could fall into its net.

Effectively, it meant the policeman's cocked ear for

---

* Trocchi is more fairly judged by his best work, the autofiction *Cain's Book* (1960), written under the 'controlled' use, self-proclaimed, of heroin.

'four-letter words' which would refer the book upwards as high as the Home Office, if necessary. In 1925, for example, the Cambridge police learned that a young lecturer at the university was intending to discuss a book called *Ulysses* by James Joyce with 'boys and girls' – i.e. his students – and had ordered copies for them from Heffers bookshop. A sales assistant had snitched.

The Home Office issued instructions. Police entered the academic's office and examined his bookshelves. The main university-serving bookshop was told, under pain of prosecution, not to stock a volume called *Ulysses* unless Homer's name were attached. The Home Secretary threatened the university senate with 'prompt criminal proceedings' if the depraving and corrupting college class were proceeded with. It wasn't.

The lecturer in the firing zone was F. R. Leavis, later a distinguished critic. And a dyed-in-the-wool Lawrentian. When I was eighteen, and myself deep into Lawrence's legitimate works, a luckless Hornsey bookseller was sentenced to two months' imprisonment for 'handling' *Lady Chatterley*. This was precisely a hundred years after the 1857 Act.

There were no more than a few hundred words in either Lawrence or Joyce warranting the police's cocked ear. Cocks being the operative word. My public library (like the British Library) had its 'poison cabinet' but had its copy of *Ulysses* buried upstairs in the 'reference library' with five pages razored out.

The 1857 Act was more minatory than active. It created a climate. There were occasional *pour encourager les autres* prosecutions – Henry Vizetelly, for example, who dared publish translations of Émile Zola in the late 1880s. *La Bête humaine* could expect no welcome on British shores – even in the naughty '90s.

Jonathan Cape suffered a financial blow with Radclyffe Hall's *The Well of Loneliness* in 1928, which had, after publication, to be withdrawn and pulped. One printed line of manifest lesbian love did it: 'That night they were not divided.' They being the main character and her lover.

Fear of prosecution, injunction, lawyers' fees, the cost of withdrawing or, worse still, pulping printed editions, rendered British publishers, as Orwell put it, generically 'gutless'. Inhibition ruled. Whether it is good or bad for literature to exist under such internal and external control is a moot point. Kingsley Amis, for example, argued that as with the Russian novel, under the Czarist office of censorship, the clumsy blue pencil drove the novelist of genius to higher levels of evasive art. Sedition and resistance will find artful channels. Look at Jane Austen.

The problem in Britain lay in the infinitely elastic word 'obscene'. The more rational French prosecuted writers, like Gustave Flaubert, for being *contre les mœurs*, which could mean 'morals' or 'current mores' – i.e. standards: not obscene (whatever that meant) but 'offensive' to the reading public, and authorities, of the day.

Works which might be thought obscene in Britain by some magistrate with nothing but porridge between his, later her, ears were killed in the womb or, as with Lawrence, Henry

Miller and Joyce, exiled to publication abroad. Domestic publishers did not dare touch them. Lawrence never lived to see *Lady Chatterley's Lover* published in England (the country which it is about), nor Joyce to see *Ulysses* published in Dublin (the city where it is entirely set).

In the US, the mailing (i.e. transporting across state lines) of 'obscene' books was a federal offence. But selling books reckoned obscene at community level were subject to multiple locally voted-in 'blue nose' regulations of the 'banned in Boston' kind. 'Published in Paris' was the only clear runway for a book judged obscene in Britain or America until the '60s.

Victorian morality, as the '60s arrived, was becoming a major cultural pain in Britain. The wily opposition backbencher Roy Jenkins (later Labour Home Secretary) saw a dripping leak in what were called the 'floodgates' – keeping, as their keepers felt, tides of filth out of the public domain.

Under Jenkins's proposed 1959 Obscene Publications Act, a book would be able to defend itself against the 'deprave and corrupt' prohibition if it could be proved to have 'literary worth'. Jenkins got his legislation through Parliament in 1959. The first test case was *Lady Chatterley's Lover*, long since 'published in Paris'.

Using the Jenkins loophole, publishers could argue, with expert witness, the 'high literary worth' which would jump them over the 1857 'deprave and corrupt' criterion. The 'acquittal of *Lady Chat*' in November 1960 did not just throw open the floodgates; it tore them down. Literature found itself in Liberty Hall.

The Jenkins Act was dishonest, opportunistic and replete with unintended consequence as regards hardest-core and criminal pornography. But it had its worthy aspect. Literature, after 1960 (the American trials of *Lady Chatterley's Lover* took place a year or so earlier, with the same effect) was, in Erica Jong's term, 'unzipped'. And it was fun to be in it.

By earlier standards, 'filth' was everywhere. But a revolution for literary freedom came with it. Virtually every item in Martin Amis's *oeuvre* would have been prosecutable or would have had to have been editorially gelded to get into print before the *Lady Chatterley* acquittal.*

In harvesting examples of contemporary triggering, I notice a telling omission. I have not come across a single example of content warning for 'obscenity'. The idea, as regards literature, has vaporised. The term, which once lay so heavy on Lawrence and Joyce, still exists but has migrated. It is now routinely affixed to the '[obscene] wealth' of Jeff Bezos, or the '[obscene] profits' of oil companies.

What is 'banned' in the 2020s in the two great Anglophone bookworlds is print which teaches or could be thought to give heart to terrorism. It is the long, continuously reopened wound of 9/11, the Hebdo 2015 massacre and the 2005 London and 2017 Manchester bombings.

One case will make the point about current book censorship in Britain. In May 2021, 53-year-old Nicholas Brock of Maidenhead was jailed for four years at Kingston-upon-Thames

---

* For more on this licentious period, see my *Offensive Literature: Decensorship in Britain, 1960–1982* (1982).

Crown Court, largely on the evidence of possessing 'manuals' (i.e. instructional books at the time freely available from Amazon) on knife fighting and making explosives.

Brock reportedly made no explosives and left no evidence of intending to blow anything up. He collected Nazi memorabilia (particularly knives – which he hung on his bedroom wall). Knives, as one of his shelves made clear, fascinated him. His interest was, it seemed, fetishistic not murderous.

The current price for the legal purchase of SS daggers on eBay is between £72 and £120. Nazi memorabilia are something of a glut on the market. There is no law against buying, owning or using them as room decoration. Carrying them in public is criminal, as is carrying a breadknife. There is no evidence of Brock carrying a knife outside his bedroom.

It was the books and reading matter Brock bought, or in two cases downloaded as PDFs, which were the main evidence brought against him in court. Pictures of his room, a pathetic little gallery of his 'collection', show it to have been excessively tidy. He lived, unmarried, with his mother, who apparently cleaned his room without traumatic consequence.

A fantasist, Brock had a certificate of membership from the KKK (not known to be active in Maidenhead). He had a framed picture of himself with a fake gun in front of a Confederate flag wearing a MAGA hat. Neither is Donald Trump big in Maidenhead. Brock's more local sympathies are indicated by a folder entitled 'Enoch Powell' containing printouts: principally the 'rivers of blood' speech, holy writ to fringe racists.

Brock belonged to no extremist organisations, neither by physical attendance at meetings nor demonstrations nor via online subscription. He had 'no interest' in far-right groups, he told the police, and 'didn't go out much'. He would seem to have been a terrorist entirely in his head, not in the streets. No grooming via the net was adduced in court. He was 'self-radicalised', the police asserted, by 'browsing online'. Browsing? Brock's was, more precisely, a kind of terrorist masturbation. Fantasy. 'Thoughtcrime' (Orwell's term) is 'nocrime'. Yet.*

It was the 'terrorist manuals' (legally purchased books or downloaded tracts) which seem to have done Brock most damage in court. Prosecutors described the 'stash' as suitable for 'an undergraduate degree' in terrorism: no university in the Western world offers such a course.

Judge Peter Lodder QC stressed when sentencing Brock's 'enthusiasm for … repulsive and toxic ideology'. Is enthusiasm a crime? Just what were the 'terrorist manuals' which were cited against him in court? There was Adolf Hitler's *Mein Kampf* (in English) and *The Klansman* by William Bradford Huie, both currently available from Amazon and AbeBooks for dirt cheap. *The Anarchist Cookbook*, a bomb-making manual, first published in 1971, is available from Amazon for £13.99. Brock had an early 2000 version, downloaded from the internet free of charge.

---

* At moment of writing, there are reports that scientific experiment has discovered, by MRI examination of brainwaves and how key words operate on them, private thought can be translated into text. The prospects are Orwellian.

He also had a copy of 'Kill or Get Killed: Riot Control Techniques, Manhandling, and Close Combat, for Police and the Military', which is freely and openly available online. He had *White Riot: The Violent Story of Combat 18*, by Nick Lowles, available from Amazon for £7.03. It is the exposé of a neo-Nazi British fringe group. The only other book mentioned in court, apparently, was *Put 'Em Down, Take 'Em Out! Knife Fighting Techniques from Folsom Prison* by 'Don Pentecost', available from Amazon (and selling well for decades) as a Kindle eBook for £2.45 – the price of half a pint of beer.

The last, by the way, has a trigger warning: 'The techniques and drills depicted in this book are extremely dangerous. It is not the intent of the author, publisher, or distributors of this book to encourage readers to attempt any of these techniques or drills without proper professional supervision and training.'

Qualified instructors in lethal knife fighting are hard to come by in Maidenhead. Nonetheless, Detective Chief Superintendent Kath Barnes, head of Counter Terrorism Policing South East, said: 'He had books which would provide techniques on how to fight, assisting someone who was potentially preparing a terrorist act.'

A protest, based on the general legal accessibility of what, as possession, was the main evidence against Brock has been sent to the Home Secretary. No response is recorded. We are nervous, it is clear, and for good reasons, about different things from the Victorians. It shows in our current laws and their practice.

The only book of literary merit in my reading lifetime which I am aware as being a 'terrorist manual' is Frederick Forsyth's *The Day of the Jackal* (1971), which instructs on how to acquire a false passport and therewith a new identity with which to cross borders and throw police off the scent. The Provisional IRA and other groups and individual criminals have found it invaluable.

PART THREE

CASE STUDIES

DICKENS RACIST! DICKENS RACIST!

Sometimes trigger warnings come with a brush and paint pot. Ian Driver daubed, on a dark night in June 2020, 'DICKENS RACIST! DICKENS RACIST!' on the Dickens House Museum in Broadstairs. For good measure, Driver attempted to black out the sign on the nearby Dickens Road. He then drove off to remind the world the next morning of Charles Dickens's racism with graffiti on Ramsgate monuments to the Great Inimitable. It was a hard night's work.

Why this crusade? Driver was an eminently respectable citizen. He had served on the Broadstairs Council for four years representing the Green Party (it is not recorded what colour paint he used to expose Dickens).

Before his trial on seven charges of criminal damage, he told the local newspaper, *Kent Live*: 'I have been campaigning for quite a long time about what I regard to be institutional racism in Thanet and Broadstairs in particular.'

The George Floyd atrocity and the tipping of the Bristol slave-trader Edward Colston's statue into the river had, he said, roused him to direct action:

> After the Black Lives Matter protests and seeing people learn their local history like the statue of Edward Colston in Bristol, I decided to do some digging into my hometown of twelve years ... Charles Dickens is celebrated in Broadstairs like a local hero and money maker just because he wrote a few books here. In reality, he was a notorious genocidal racist and should be depicted as such. That's the real Dickens.

He pleaded innocent to all charges, enabling him to make his denunciation more public under witness privilege. At the trial on 2 August 2021, he was found guilty of all charges and fined £1,400. He got his headlines cheap.

That Dickens the *man* (the word is important, as distinct from 'Dickens the *author*') was all that Driver claimed, and more, is no secret. On his part, Dickens made every effort that everything really personal in his life should be kept from posterity – the 'burglars and grave robbers' as Henry James called them. Dickens made a huge bonfire of his letters on 3 September 1860. His children, who had brought the papers out in a convoy of baskets, roasted potatoes, legend has it, in the embers of their father's secret life. Most burningly, all reference to his current affair with Nelly Ternan – the 'Invisible Woman', as Claire Tomalin's biography entitles her. Dickens, on that September afternoon, did his damndest to make her so.

But he could not call back and incinerate all his private correspondence. Modern scholarship has both served and ill-served Dickens by printing, in thirteen breeze-blocked volumes, tens of thousands of his surviving letters.

As regards his attitudes on race, the letters cast light into dark places. Dickens reveals himself as abusive of Irish and Scottish Britons. The Welsh are beneath his notice. As for African Americans after the Civil War, the abolition of slavery and enfranchisement, he chortled at 'the melancholy absurdity of giving these people votes' which would 'glare out of every roll of their eyes, chuckle in their mouths, and bump in their heads'. The reference to bumps is phrenological. Their benighted race didn't have the brains to vote. Around 750,000 Americans had died for an absurdity. That absurdity being the treating of black people like human beings.

Dickens's most virulent racism boiled over in the year of the 'Sepoy Mutiny', now more correctly called the 'Indian Uprising' or 'Indian Rebellion' of 1857. It was some months before detailed news reached London. When it did, Dickens exploded. He applauded the captured Indian 'rebels' being strapped on the mouths of artillery and blasted to kingdom come. He commissioned an article on the hideous practice for his tuppenny journal *Household Words* entitled 'Blown Away!' The article's author described, in faithful Dickensian floridity, the mist of 'atomised' blood and flesh fragments descending on the watching victors and the 'natives' forcibly gathered to learn a message they would never forget. It added to the relish that this disgusting mode of execution denied the Hindus last rites – important in their faith.

Dickens wrote to a banker friend later in 1857:

I wish I were Commander in Chief over [India]! I would address that Oriental character which must be powerfully spoken to, in something like the following placard, which should be vigorously translated into all native dialects, 'I, The Inimitable, holding this office of mine, and firmly believing that I hold it by the permission of Heaven and not by the appointment of Satan, have the honour to inform you Hindoo gentry that it is my intention, with all possible avoidance of unnecessary cruelty and with all merciful swiftness of execution, *to exterminate the Race* from the face of the earth, which disfigured the earth with the late abominable atrocities.'*

A 'Hindoo' Prime Minister of England, AD 2022? One wishes Dickens were alive to see it.

One could stack the evidence mountain high that Dickens the man (NB 'man') was racist most of the time and genocidal at some times. One needs no wall and paint pot. It's all there in print.

But (recalling Ian Driver's felonious fury) why is Dickens's crass imperial racism so widely ignored? Say 'Dickensian' and

---

* My stress.

the literate person will think of Tiny Tim blessing us all, Mr Pickwick in his habitual pickle, Oliver asking for more and Little Nell dying in a shower of tears. Not that awful dismemberment of Indians by cannon shell.

The answer lies in deep waters. The first, and most important, reason for Dickens's racism not being registered is because it is not to be found overtly in his novels. And the biographies downplay it. Other than the arrant antisemitism in *Oliver Twist* (which, to his credit, he went some way to correcting), looking for racism in Dickens's fiction is short commons as it is not, for example, in that of his rival William Makepeace Thackeray or 'the Lesser Thackeray', Anthony Trollope.* Dickens the novelist is, on the evidence, different from Dickens the man. But which, one may ask, is the truer Dickens?

The other reason for Dickens's pro-imperial racism being generally blanked away is us. It seems we (at least many of us) really don't want to know. Put another way, we know but don't want to be reminded. It doesn't fit into our larger mindsets. A YouGov poll of 2014 discovered that, sixty-four years after India's independence, 60 per cent of Britons remained proud of the British Empire and almost 50 per cent thought the empire had made the former colonies better off. Nowhere more than in that jewel in the imperial crown, India (on the subject of

---

* I deal with Dickens's antisemitism elsewhere in these pages and Thackeray's anti-black racism in the epilogue. Trollope, after visiting Australia, believed the Indigenous Australians ('Aborigines') should die out for the convenience of their white colonists. It was the best service they could offer.

jewels, one may note that the Koh-i-Noor is yet to be returned to its rightful, subcontinental, owners).

How to account for this counterfactual mythopoeia? Nostalgia? The phantom limb phenomenon in which the lost arm still tingles, hurts and feels? Folk memory? It was, if polls were to be believed, a national blind spot. A willed blind spot.

Two years later, in 2016, came the Brexit referendum. Surveys discovered that at this later date, some 50 per cent of 'Leave' voters felt the empire was something to be proud of; a mere 20 per cent of 'Remain' voters felt the same way. Dickens, one fancies, would have been up on the hustings with Boris Johnson roaring to get Brexit done and bring back 'sovereignty' (what sovereign? Victoria?).

The Labour Party manifesto for the 2019 general election promised that if the party came to power, it would 'conduct an audit of the impact of Britain's colonial legacy to understand our contribution to the dynamics of violence and insecurity across regions previously under British colonial rule'.

It cut no ice. Labour suffered the worst loss in its history. The 'audit' never happened. A year later, 27 per cent of the British people said they would like to have 'their' empire back.

Abolish Dickens? Ian Driver will need a lot more paint.

MOLLY RUSSELL AND *RIVERDALE*

Molly Russell was, as the world and her parents saw her, a bright, happy fourteen-year-old being brought up safely in an outer London middle-class family. Like her peers, she had a personal phone and private bedroom computer. They were passports to an electronic world in which her parents did not follow. Worlds of knowledge, peer communication and popular culture, parents like them commonly assume.

Writing about her after her death, Molly's father, Ian, described her as an ostensibly 'positive, happy, bright young lady who was indeed destined to do good'. It was true that in the last year of her life, she had become 'more withdrawn' and spent more time in her room. But in company, her parents remembered, she was normally in 'good spirits', along with the normal early teenage 'mood swings'.

On the evening of 20 November 2017, Molly and her family watched an episode of the new series of *I'm a Celebrity... Get Me Out of Here!* after supper and before Molly's bedtime. The reality programme was set in the Australian bush that year; for laughs at those 'celebrities' subjected to horrific 'bushtucker grub'. The humour was cloacal.

As Molly's mother, Janet, later told the police: 'Everybody's behaviour was normal.' It was Monday; Molly had school next day. At around seven the next morning, Mrs Russell went to Molly's bedroom and found her daughter dead. Inquests where there are inexplicable circumstances are routinely painfully delayed. In Molly Russell's case, the e-data was mountainous and the police were slow to plough through it all with forensic attention. Need for information from internet content providers slowed things to snail speed. More so, since Molly had, apparently, run proxy accounts: common among teenagers.

It was not until September 2022 that the inquest was held.

Molly would have been nineteen. The Russells had legal assistance and had been publicising what they believed had driven their daughter to self-destruction. In the broadest sense, it was the internet – that dangerous contemporary Narnia on the other side of the wardrobe door. Ian Russell told the court he now knew – he hadn't then – Molly had been sucked into 'the bleakest of worlds … It's a world I don't recognise. It's a ghetto of the online world that once you fall into it, the algorithm means you can't escape it and it keeps recommending more content. You can't escape it.'

Other young people in Molly's peer group were in their own ghettos of anorexia, intropunitive self-harm, *Weltschmerz*. All could cross the bridge from fantasy to real life. Molly's ghetto was suicide. The means were as easily accessible on the net as cooking recipes.

The 'bleak world' is self-archiving. One datum stood out: 'Of 16,300 pieces of content saved, liked or shared by Molly on Instagram in the six months before she died, 2,100 were related to suicide, self-harm and depression.'

The Metropolitan Police scrutinised Molly's phone records. It yielded tens of thousands of pages for the Russells and their lawyers.

There were, it gradually emerged, two Mollys. One was the girl at the dinner table and goggleboxing network TV with the family on the living room sofa; the other was alone with her phone and keyboard in her bedroom. The other Molly gave herself the Twitter handle 'Idfc_nomore' – 'I don't fucking care no more'. It sounds like bravado; it wasn't.

The coroner's verdict was epochal. Molly had not – as is the routine escape line in such cases – killed herself while 'the balance of the mind was disturbed'. She had died 'from an act of self-harm while suffering from depression and the negative effects of online content'. Her mind had been poisoned.

Her online existence was not entirely negative. In her Twitter profile, she headed her description with the slogan: 'Harry Potter is Life'. But the great hoax of social media is its false milieu of 'chatroom' intimacy. On 15 October 2017, a few weeks before her death, Molly tweeted J. K. Rowling: 'My mind has been full of suicidal thoughts for a while but reading Harry Potter and the world you created has been my escape.'

She, poor girl, did not in the event escape. Her tweet was lost in the thousands Rowling receives every day. Poignantly, Molly believed she could talk more openly to a Twitter account than to her parents or any responsible person at her school.

In addition to steeping herself in Hogwarts, Molly watched the American TV series *Riverdale*. The programme's history is bizarre. It began in the 1940s as a comic book narrative about an all-American kid called Archie who lives in the fictitious town of Riverdale. He could have been played by the young Mickey Rooney.

This seed grew by comic book adaptation and novelisation into the hugely successful 2017-launched TV series in which teenagers, still living in mythic Riverdale, inhabit a world of fantasised sex and violence. There is in early episodes a central suicide theme, along with teen murder and a paedophile affair between a fifteen-year-old student and an adult teacher.

The series (available on Netflix) is compellingly well done and noir. The parental content warning website Common Sense Media labels it an 'awful show and extremely inappropriate' going on to explain:

> This show is terrible and extremely inappropriate for children and young teens … Riverdale glamorizes a sexual relationship between a teacher and a 15-year-old high school student, features a shower sex scene between two teenagers and a scene of a high school girl performing a strip tease in a bar full of classmates and adult men, normalizes drug labs and drug use, and promotes unhealthy family dynamics and unrealistic relationships.

Molly Russell, recall, was fourteen when watching *Riverdale*. It's the nature of such series' appeal that they draw in younger-than-aimed-at viewers. One of the series' fan sites ('The Mighty') has contributions from adherents occasionally urging that *Riverdale* be triggered – particularly for younger viewers and episodes containing suicide plots.

Molly Russell identified strongly with Lili Reinhart, who plays Betty Cooper in the series, the first of which premiered on 26 January 2017. In May that first year, Reinhart 'ranted' (her word) on her Twitter feed about depression in the month dedicated to progress in treating teenage depression. Reinhart wrote: '*Riverdale* came into my life when I was going through the worst depression I had ever experienced.' It had, she said, kicked in when she was at middle school, aged fourteen, and ravaged her ever since (she was born in 1996). Her sense of being out of place at school 'allowed me to further sink into this world where I was by myself and isolating myself'.

To mark World Suicide Prevention Day on 10 September 2017, two months before Molly's death, Reinhart posted a picture of herself on Instagram holding up the free 1-800 phone number for the National Suicide Prevention Helpline.

Reinhart, who was already a major hit on *Riverdale*, now had 3 million followers – including Molly Russell – who retweeted her. Molly did not phone up the suicide hotline but wrote directly to Reinhart: 'I can't take it no more, I need someone but I can't reach out to anyone I love I just can't take it.' As with Rowling, she did not hear back for the same reason.

In their daughters' memory, the Russells and friends set up the Molly Rose Foundation. Its aim is suicide prevention, targeted towards young people 'under the age of 25 … MRF wants to help reach those at risk of suicide and connect them to the help, support, and practical advice they need.'

Obviously, the one thing needful was what would be, if it happened, the biggest triggering operation in cultural history. It formed itself as the British Online Safety Bill. Alas, at the time of writing, it has not yet managed to stumble its way through the maze of parliamentary legislation into efficient control of the World Wide Web.

'BALLY SILLY', DON'T A FELLOW HAVETERTHINK?

The Times, on 17 April 2023, broke the news to the nation that

'P. G. "Plum" Wodehouse is the latest author to have their work altered after a publishing house edited several Jeeves and Wooster books as part of an effort to remove "unacceptable" prose'. Plum, apparently, was depipped.

The books at issue were archetypal Wodehouse: *Right Ho, Jeeves* and *Thank You, Jeeves*, both first published in 1934. They represent the writer's first efforts in full-length fiction. More 'edited' Wodehousiana is to come, evidently cleansing the whole corpus. The publisher was the Anglo-American Penguin Random House combine. Archetypally English in his fiction, Wodehouse spent most of his adult life in the US. *The Times* understood the future revised editions had

> passages reworked or removed ... to strip [the novels] of language that modern audiences might find offensive ... The publisher has also included trigger warnings to revised editions stating that Wodehouse's themes and characters may be 'outdated'. Among the examples of changes cited is a racial term used in *Right Ho, Jeeves* to describe a 'minstrel of the old school'. It has been removed. In *Thank You, Jeeves*, whose plot concerns a minstrel troupe, numerous racial terms have been removed or altered, both in dialogue spoken by the characters in the book and from first-person narration in the voice of Bertie [Bertram Wooster, Esquire].

For some in 2023, Bertie's omnicompetent personal valet might seem obnoxiously 'outdated' as a classist example of English servitude to an upper-class do-nothing (his club is proudly called 'the Drones'). But Penguin Random House's cited erasures were specifically of 'racial terms'.

One of the books *The Times* mentions,* *Right Ho, Jeeves*, is available, free online, textually intact and word-searchable, on Gutenberg. Wodehouse, who died in 1975, is now in the public domain in the US but not, until 2045, in the UK.

In *Right Ho, Jeeves*, there is only one N-word usage: 'When I was able to see clearly once more, I perceived that Gussie was now seated. He had his hands on his knees, with his elbows out at right angles, like a nigger minstrel of the old school about to ask Mr Bones why a chicken crosses the road.'

Thank You, Jeeves, by contrast, is, as regards racism, wholly offensive – hence Gutenberg's discreet cancellation of the novel. Penguin Random House is evidently made of sterner stuff.

The narrative opens with Bertie having become infatuated with the banjolele. A hybrid instrument, it became popular in the 1920s. Strung like the Hawaiian Islands' ukulele, it was crossed with the banjo – an instrument invented by American slaves (typically with old cigar boxes and cat gut), denied as they were orchestral instruments or choral performance other than in their church. They made one of the greatest American art forms, the blues, out of debris.

The banjolele was made famous in Britain by George Formby, who was a virtuoso on the instrument and supreme-ly popular in the '30s and '40s. Everyone loved the gormless

---

* Titles of the multiple reprints of the two novels discussed here sometimes add an exclamation mark, sometimes not. The invisible '!' is ubiquitous in dialogue in the novels.

Wigan working-class lad (who offstage was as smart as they come). He occasionally went blackface.

By 1934 and the publication of the two Wodehouse novels, Formby was a superstar of the music hall boards, shellac 78s and the 'flicks'. His highlight was always a dazzling banjolele number. He wrote many of his own songs, which were witty and occasionally naughty – viz, 'Fanlight Fanny', 'When I'm Cleaning Windows', 'With My Little Stick of Blackpool Rock'.

Thank You, Jeeves never mentions Formby by name, but that Bertie is obsessed to the point of mania with the banjolele makes the point. So manic, and imperfect, a performer is Bertram Wooster, Esq., that his London neighbours in Berkeley Square (where, according to the ballad, nightingales sing) rise up to complain at the caterwaul.

Bertie cadges a cottage on the country estate of his Drones pal 'Chuffy'. Lord Reginald Chuffnell, according to Debrett. Jeeves, no fan of nightingales in their natural habitat, departs Bertie's service for that of said Chuffy, who is angling to marry into American millions. He loves Pauline, the daughter of J. Washburn Stoker for whom millions are small change. Bertie has also been distantly romantically involved with the heiress. The aristocratic classes of England, after the First World War supertax and the 1929 financial crash, were on their uppers and scrounging – in an upper-crust way.

The plot gets knotted. While strumming in the backwoods with a comically drunken Jeeves replacement, Bertie is told by Chuffy: 'There's a troupe of nigger minstrels down there [i.e. his part of the country] this year. You could study their technique.' The term is – although this is not to defend it – descriptive. 'N***er minstrels' were white blackface minstrels playing to exclusively white audiences. Central to their repertoire were the songs of (white) Stephen Foster, many of which were 'comically' racist such as 'Camptown Races' (1850):

> De Camptown ladies sing dis song, Doo-dah! doo-dah!
> De Camptown race-track five miles long, Oh, doo-dah day!
> I come down dah wid my hat caved in, Doo-dah! doo-dah!
> I go back home wid a pocket full of tin, Oh, doo-dah day!

It was sung, as one of his standards, along with 'My Mammy' by Al Jolson, in blackface, in the 1930s. Wodehouse would have heard it many times.

'Coloured minstrels', by contrast, were authentically black performers performing for exclusively black audiences. Sometimes with white gatecrashers. They were, unlike their blackfaced white counterparts, genuinely creative, with strong links to gospel hymnology. That, in turn, is the cradle of – for example – Aretha Franklin and Tina Turner. Minstrelsy, along with the blues and ragtime (eventually rock and roll), was an original African American musical art form: profitably misappropriated by white artists like Jolson and the above-discussed G. H. Elliott, 'the Chocolate Coloured Coon'. Wooster himself uses the N-word half a dozen times about the visiting minstrels who never appear.

Bertie, by a series of comic misadventures, finds himself kidnapped on J. Washburn Stoker's palatial yacht, held hostage until he, not Chuffy, marries Pauline. A shotgun wedding, Yankee style, looms. The black minstrels are due to come and entertain the other passengers. How will Bertie get out of this almighty mess?

Jeeves, ever Bertie's solve-all 'man' (though technically now in Chuffy's employ), comes to the rescue: 'I have a small tin of boot polish here, sir,' he says. 'I brought it with me in anticipation of this move. It would be a simple task to apply it to your face and hands in such a manner as to create the illusion, should you encounter Mr Stoker, that you were a member of this troupe of negroid entertainers.'

Jeeves uses the term 'negro' and its derivative several times. Never the N-word.

With Jeeves's help, Bertie makes good his escape. But shoe polish, unlike stage greasepaint, is deuced hard to remove from a fellow's phiz. He can't come by petrol or butter to do it. He is forced to duck and dodge like a runaway slave. Interesting thought.

Finally, driven by hunger, he forces an entry to Chuffy's stately home via (shame! shame!) the tradesman's entrance. The door is opened by a scullery maid who falls into fits, screaming on the floor, 'frothing at the mouth' at the sight of him.*

It provokes deep thoughts, not entirely to Bertie's discredit:

---

* She has, we suppose, being a country girl, never seen a black face before but has heard terrifying stories about 'savages'. The black population of the United Kingdom is estimated at around 50,000 out of 45 million in the 1930s.

I had never realised before what an important part one's complexion plays in life ... I mean to say, Bertram Wooster with merely a pretty tan calling at the back door of Chuffnell Hall would have been received with respect and deference ... But purely and simply because there happened to be a little boot polish on my face, here was this female tying herself in knots on the doormat and throwing fits up and down the passage.

Complications are ingeniously unravelled. Jeeves's replacement drunkenly burns Bertie's cottage down and with it the banjolele, which was his reason for being there. He can return to his natural habitat, Mayfair, and drone with his fellow wastrels and strum no more.

Offensive in its original form as it is, *Thank You, Jeeves* remains significant as evidence of cultural movement. The novel's 'minstrel plot' points, three decades into the future, towards the last ripples of a historically sudden sea change in British racial attitudes.

The Black and White Minstrel Show, featuring not black minstrels but full blackface white performers, ran weekly on BBC TV, from 1958 to 1978. Its average viewing figure was 10 million; it rose to a peak of 21 million in 1964. The population of Britain was 54 million at that time. The programme was black and white TV until 1967. Stephen Foster and Al Jolson tributes were favourite items. A whole December 1960 show, highlighting these two, can be found, free of charge, on YouTube.

Lenny Henry (now Sir Lenny Henry) was the first and only authentically black performer to appear on the show. Initially a teenager, he stayed with it for almost five years. In an interview with *The Times* in 2021, he recalled his weekly discomfort: 'People used to say Lenny was the only one who didn't need make-up. It was half funny once, but to hear that every day for five years was a bit of a pisser.'

The BBC airily brushed off any protest, arguing that the show was good family fare; look at the viewing figures. George Melly wittily pointed out that throwing Christians to the lions was good family fare in ancient Rome.

The 1991 UK census was the first to include a question on ethnicity. It recorded that the black population in England (half of it concentrated, as tight communities, in London) amounted to 1.6 per cent of the whole 57 million. With that now considerable and growing figure in mind, along with *Thank You, Jeeves*'s minstrelsy, there was a strangely race-centred event in May 1991; the year in which the RAF bombed Baghdad and the IRA bombed Downing Street.

ITV had launched a highly successful, BAFTA-winning weekly hour-long series called *Jeeves and Wooster* in 1990. It ran until 1993. It was situational comedy, each instalment based on (more or less faithfully) different Wodehouse narratives. The series offered a tonally pitch perfect send up of the English class system. Hugh Laurie (Bertie) and Stephen Fry (Jeeves) played the title roles. Both were public-school educated (Eton and Uppingham) and knew the social types they were guying.

ITV decided to do *Thank You, Jeeves*, retitled 'Kidnapped', as the fifth episode of the second series on 12 May 1991. The first half of the narrative follows the novel but without the banjolele or any mention of it. There are grossly unWodehousian changes, however, to the minstrel plot.

As rescripted, the Drones en masse resolve to promote their pal Chuffy's wedding to Pauline. To do so, and rescue the kidnapped Bertie in the process, they black up pretending to be the minstrels who have been hired to entertain on J. Washburn Stoker's yacht. Aided, as in the novel, with Jeeves's boot polish, Bertie escapes among the black throng of banjo (not banjolele) players. It all ends up with Bertie and the Drones being arrested only to be discharged by the sitting magistrate who turns out to be none other than Chuffy – free at last to claim Pauline.

It's half-baked. The blacking-up of a dozen Hooray Henries almost gets by as comic licence, but it testifies, some might think, to an ineradicable vein of racialism in the English psyche. This, recall, is 1991. The programme has most recently reappeared, in full, for free on YouTube as part of a charity drive for Ukraine in its war against Russia. Apparently, Britons still find it funny. Four per cent of them (by the 2021 census figures) probably don't.

GONE WITH THE WIND LIVES AGAIN

Following a lead in the *Telegraph*, on 2 April 2023 the Mail-Online splashed the news that '*Gone with the Wind* is slapped with trigger warning by its own publisher with message at front of new edition branding it "harmful" because of its "racist and stereotypical depictions".

It wasn't news for anyone who had read the novel unblinded by the 1939 sugar-coated film version that Margaret Mitchell's novel was horrifically racist. The fact that Rhett Butler rides of a night with the Ku Klux Klan (Clark Gable doesn't in the movie) was no secret: it's there in the 1936 text. Imprisoned by the victorious Yankees, after the Civil War, Rhett (in the novel) pleads innocent of shooting a freed African American. He gets off. Later he confesses to Scarlett O'Hara:

> No, now that I am free of the toils, I'll frankly admit that I'm as guilty as Cain. I did kill the nigger. He was uppity to a lady, and what else could a Southern gentleman do? And while I'm confessing, I must admit that I shot a Yankee cavalryman after some words in a barroom. I was not charged with that peccadillo, so perhaps some other poor devil has been hanged for it, long since.

The film spares Clark Gable that gentlemanly admission.

Scarlett admires the southern politesse of her gentleman callers. *Uncle Tom's Cabin* – with its noble resident – is, however, not for her, the southern belle. On the one occasion that she is described as entering one, 'the faint niggery smell' of the slave cabin nauseates her.

There are 104 uses of the N-word in the narrative. The novel is e-printed, free of charge and word searchable, on

Gutenberg's Australian sister site. To get the taste of the whole, look for a few minutes at the 104 usages.

The last words from Scarlett – 'After all, tomorrow is another day' – predict that the south will rise again, if not this time on black shoulders. Born in 1900 surrounded by old timers who remember the good old days, Margaret Mitchell was, reportedly, ten years old before she realised the Confederates had lost the Civil War. It took a long time – until 1964 – to pull the deep south in any way substantially out of its past.* Margaret Mitchell was never pulled.

What to do with this novel? Hollywood, under the management of MGM (*ars gratia artis* under Leo the Lion being its symbol) and producer David Selznick, knew exactly what to do. Lie in Technicolor. One of the early script and screen-play writers was F. Scott Fitzgerald, whose scenario went full Gatsby on the antebellum first half of the narrative:

> To suggest the romance of the old South immediately ... I'd like to see a two or three-minute montage of the most beautiful pre-war shots imaginable ... I'd like to see ... negroes singing ... Then we could go into the story of disappointed love, betraying overseers, toiling negroes and quarrelling girls.

No smelly cabins or uppity black people for Scott. MGM decided to go halfway with his 'suggestion'. Selznick and Mitchell

---

* The date of the US 1964 Civil Rights Act.

locked horns over the N-word. She wanted a realistic depiction of the south – and a spray of its most offensive dialect. Selznick, after consulting African American spokespeople, nixed her demand absolutely. They had paid Mitchell $50,000 and the property was now theirs. Read the contract.

Without going all the way with Fitzgerald (Selznick, incidentally, let him go; he was now a Hollywood hack, not a great novelist), the film romanticised the novel and, with it, the most self-defining moment in post-independence US history. White crime on black – which was what slavery was – was replaced by white crime on white: the burning of Atlanta, the film's money shot. The old south was rendered beautiful, all balls and belles and 'southern gentleman'. A beautiful pack of lies. It was, in its day, and in box office receipts, the most popular film ever put on screen.

The hard-nosed decision on *Gone with the Wind* the novel would be to let it now sink into unread oblivion. Not give a damn, my dear, about it any more – to echo Rhett Butler's famous last words in the film. That, however, would be a mistake. Mitchell's novel, despite its *parti pris* for the slave-owning past of the south, is analytic popular history. She knew the antebellum and postbellum south from the constant, nostalgic and angry tale-telling of her elders.

Her novel does not romanticise the old south, Fitzgerald style: it tells it like it was. Take the following passage (Tom Slattery is a 'poor white' sharecropper):

The sight of Tom Slattery dawdling on his neighbors'

porches, begging cotton seed for planting or a side of bacon to 'tide him over', was a familiar one. Slattery hated his neighbors with what little energy he possessed, sensing their contempt beneath their courtesy, and especially did he hate 'rich folks' uppity niggers'. The house negroes of the County considered themselves superior to white trash, and their unconcealed scorn stung him, while their more secure position in life stirred his envy. By contrast with his own miserable existence, they were well-fed, well-clothed and looked after in sickness and old age. They were proud of the good names of their owners and, for the most part, proud to belong to people who were quality, while he was despised by all.

All the white trash had was their skin. And slavery was necessary to make its being white worthwhile. Mitchell depicts a precise hierarchy of African Americans under slavery: house slaves and yard slaves; country slaves and town slaves; 'trashy free issue former slaves' (those given antebellum freedom passes); and postbellum, freedmen former slaves – thanks to Yankee 'former slave lovers'. All the lexicon and hierarchies of slavery and slavers is precisely notated, with the foul terminology (euphemised here). Sickening but historically evidential.

During her lifetime, Margaret Mitchell's novel was advertised as 'the book which has sold more copies than any other except the Bible'. That lifetime was short. She was mowed down by a taxi in her native Atlanta, aged forty-eight, in 1949. She left only the one published novel behind her. So too did

Harper Lee – *To Kill a Mockingbird*. Lee lived to the age of eighty-nine, in deep southern Alabama, dying in 2016.

Had Mitchell lived to Lee's age, *Gone with the Wind* would have been, by the post-mortem protection of authorial copyright for seventy years, hers and her estate's until 2060. As it was, *GWTW* (as fan sites label it) came into the public domain in 2020 when, evidently, Pan Macmillan resolved on their new edition.

The decision, for a publishing house in the 2020s, was awkward. They could trim the text of all the most offensive items. Or they could beat the critics to the punch and trigger the novel themselves.

They went for trigger double-plus. The work was prefaced with a solemn warning that 'readers could find "racist" aspects of the era "hurtful or indeed harmful"'. Pan Macmillan, they declared, had decided not to remove 'objectionable content' but this should not be taken as 'an endorsement' of the book. The content contained, they further warned:

> The romanticisation of a shocking era in our history [and] the representation of unacceptable practices, racist and stereotypical depictions and troubling themes, characterisation, language and imagery … We want to alert readers that there may be hurtful or indeed harmful phrases and terminology that were prevalent at the time this novel was written and which are true to the context of the historical setting of this novel.

Not yet finished with machine-gunning themselves in the

foot, Pan Macmillan commissioned the British historical fiction writer Philippa Gregory, famed for her novels on the English Civil War, to write a new foreword in the latest version, laying out the 'white supremacist' aspects of the book. One of her comments was prophylactically released by the publisher: '*Gone with the Wind* tells us, unequivocally, that African people are not of the same species as white people … This is the lie that spoils the novel.' As the *Mail* records: 'Pan Macmillan explained that Gregory was chosen, as a white writer, to pen the essay in order to avoid inflicting "emotional labour" on a minority writer.'

THE UNDERGROUND RAILROAD

In August 2022, *The Times* reported that the 2017 prize-winning novel *The Underground Railroad* by Colson Whitehead had been 'permanently removed' from a course at Essex University 'because of concerns about graphic depictions of slavery'.

The Underground Railroad is a distinguished work ('terrific' was President Obama's verdict) by a distinguished author. Colson Whitehead had won NBA and Pulitzer awards and, in the UK, Booker listing. In 2002, aged thirty-three, he received a MacArthur 'Genius Grant' (half a million dollars no strings attached). Scurrilous legend had it that male geniuses were asked (but not by the foundation) to denote a sample of their semen for the future good of humankind.

The Underground Railroad (2016) was Whitehead's sixth

novel. It can be seen as homage to two literary forebears. Primary is Margaret Atwood who, in *The Handmaid's Tale* (1985), departed from her habitual realism to protest against patriarchal oppression with the borrowed devices of science fiction. Her novel scooped up a Hugo and a Nebula – twin prize sci-fi pinnacles. It took thirty-two years, and the 2017 TV series, fully to appreciate what Atwood had done and how she had empowered fiction by her trans-genre hybridity.

The other plausible influence on Whitehead is Octavia E. Butler, who wedded realistic depiction of antebellum slavery with Wellsian time travel in *Kindred*. Butler's abrupt genre switches, from realism to sci-fi, finds a parallel in *The Underground Railroad*.*

The first sixty pages of *The Underground Railroad* merit the above word 'graphic'. Whitehead acknowledges Frederick Douglass, Harriet Jacobs and Harriet Tubman as authenticating sources. The narrative's central character is a young woman, Cora, a slave on a Georgia cotton plantation. Her oppressive masters are white male rapists with a love of the whip.

Like other African American novelists, all the way back to Ralph Ellison (author of *Invisible Man*), Whitehead found himself awkwardly positioned: writing, as he was, as a black author about historical black experiences – with all the sensory stimuli of fiction – for an overwhelmingly white readership.

At one point on her later runaway travels, Cora finds herself

---

* *Kindred* is discussed later, pp. 186–8.

presented as an exhibit in a museum, a living waxwork, depicting a wholly fictitious version of black life. White noses are pressed against the glass gawping at her.

The novel's prelude is hyper-realistic and, in the context of an English university in 2022, abrasively so. *The Underground Railroad* specifically indicts the Bank of England and Britain's textile industry as complicit to the crime of American slavery.

There is a blazingly angry moment in *The Underground Railroad* when Whitehead steps out of the novel to speak as a historian, via Martin, a white man sheltering Cora:

> As with everything in the south, it started with cotton. The ruthless engine of cotton required its fuel of African bodies … More slaves led to more cotton, which led to more money to buy more land to farm more cotton. Even with the termination of the slave trade, in less than a generation the numbers were untenable … Whites outnumbered slaves two to one in North Carolina, but in Louisiana and Georgia the populations neared parity. Just over the border in South Carolina, the number of blacks surpassed that of whites by more than a hundred thousand.

The extraordinary explosion of the black slave population in the decades before the Civil War was not by importation of human beings from Africa: that transaction was hugely wasteful – an average third of the cargo was lost at sea. More profitable was a gigantic, plantation-based breeding programme creating what was the world's first human battery-farming success story. Whitehead's account of the sophisticated crimes of slavery is harrowing.

Without warning, after its realistic prelude, the novel jerks, wholesale, into sci-fi. *The Underground Railroad's* railroad, it emerges, is not a disorganised network of trails and safe houses run by evangelical whites but an actual subterranean transport rail and steam system, built (of course) by black labour. There is no regular timetable, but it links southern departure stations, via various stops, to the destination station, vaguely called 'the north'.

Along with the sci-fi and fantasy twist, the narrative becomes picaresque chronicling Cora's various stops in North and South Carolina, Tennessee and Indiana. At each station, she encounters different aspects of white on black savagery: in one place are 'slave catchers' who find human prey a sporting challenge and cut off ears for trophy necklaces; elsewhere pseudo-benign concentration camps; there is one place where unknowing black people are infected with syphilis 'in the interest of medical science'.* Another has put in practice black genocide. Racism has its varieties: all based on the historical fact that black lives and black hurt don't matter.

The *Mail* followed up *The Times*' story and elicited an angry response from Essex University: 'It is completely untrue and misleading to say *Underground Railroad* has been banned or blacklisted. *Underground Railroad* is available in our library

---

* Alluding to the vile 'Tuskegee Experiment of Untreated Syphilis' of 1932 using 600 black male subjects.

and remains an option for inclusion on future reading lists in relevant modules.'

What, precisely, was the course from which Whitehead's novel was 'permanently removed'? David Kernohan, the deputy editor at the 'tertiary education consultant' firm Wonkhe, offered the answer.*

The Essex course in contention was a third-year (i.e. final) undergraduate module, 'The Beginning of a Novel', offered within the department of literature, film and theatre studies. It was a creative writing course in which 'students will learn how to devise and plan their own novel through the reading and study of a selection of other novels'.

One draws an obvious conclusion. *The Underground Railroad* brought too much US baggage with it for aspirant UK writers to draw useful tuition from. It had been shuffled out to make room for something more appropriately tuitional.

OLIVER TWIST: 'FAGIN DOESN'T COUNT'

In late January 2022, the *Mail on Sunday* took a tabloid page for a splash piece entitled, in banner headline, 'PLEASE SIR, I WANT LESS!' Royal Holloway University, readers learned, over their weekend breakfast, had triggered *Oliver Twist* on a Victorian literature, art and culture MA (Master of Arts) course ('MA' is nowadays universally used to avoid the term

---

* Wonkhe, founded in 2011 by 'wonk' Mark Leach, offers 'a range of bespoke services to private clients, universities, sector agencies, students' unions and others'. As the name implies, it is a think tank which carries its youth aggressively.

'Master'; 'Bachelor of Arts' and 'BA' ditto). That level of course is open only to students who have earned a first degree. The class would normally be into their twenties, of all backgrounds, with a sprinkling of 'mature' students.

The *Mail* article provoked 1,300 online comments, virtually all contemptuous, and close on a thousand shares to stir, doubtless, a snigger or two. Chris Hastings, the author of the article, was the *Mail*'s Savonarola of current triggering vanities. He's good at it. Another fine mess British universities had got themselves into was his theme.

Hastings had uncovered this latest egregious wokery by a freedom of information request. Royal Holloway, readers will recall, is where the hero in Dan Brown's *The Da Vinci Code* discovers interestingly unknown things about Jesus (the Bible, incidentally, has been profusely triggered).

When questioned by Hastings, a primed Royal Holloway spokesperson defended the decision: *Oliver Twist* had been triggered for its 'themes of child abuse, domestic violence and racial prejudice'. It was a university's pastoral duty to warn students of 'potentially sensitive topics which could cause them anxiety or distress, perhaps as a consequence of past experience'.

Dickens's book, as the *Mail on Sunday* countered, 'has inspired an Oscar-winning musical, a Disney cartoon film and countless family-friendly TV and film adaptations ... Sir David Lean's big screen adaptation in 1948 has a U certificate.' That British Board of Film Classification letter meant children of any age could watch it. Many of whom, like me, had been bombed out of their homes. I bore the strain aged nine, man-fully, despite Alec Guinness's grotesque prosthetic nose.

One sniffs something not said in the Royal Holloway affair. Elephants and rooms. The reason for the university's apparent pusillanimity is, one suspects, something seriously awkward about Dickens. In a word, 'Jews': not come out loud with by Royal Holloway but throbbing radioactively beneath the said. The trigger warning needs some unpeeling to get down to the core issue for triggering.

Royal Holloway University (originally 'College') is an or-ganic part of London University whose total student body is currently the size of a small town. University College London (UCL) is London University's *fons et origo*. Founded in 1826, its novelty was in admitting students, and employing teachers, of all faiths. UCL, from the start, welcomed Jews and gave Hebrew-language Jewish studies departmental status. Oxbridge, true to its monastic heritage, was strictly Anglican in culture, statutes, practice and regulation. And its antisemitism. Yar-mulkas in Bloomsbury; gowns and mortar boards in Oxford. Not until 1856 were male Jews admitted as students, and not until 1871 could Jews hold fellowships (tenured posts) there.

University College, then London University, received its royal charter (i.e. it became a real university) in 1836. *Oliver Twist* began serialising, to runaway success, in 1837. Dickens, at the time, was living in Doughty Street, a few hundred yards from University College. He would have seen Jewish students every day he walked the streets (which he did, furiously) and, quite likely, Britain's and UCL's first professor of Hebrew studies, Hyman Hurwitz.

The Judaic tradition at UCL remains vibrant. The current Jewish student society opens its website with the greeting 'Hello, we're the UCL JSOC. We're the largest JSOC in London and the reason our university is sometimes known as "JEW-CL"!'

Twenty-first-century anti-Zionist protest, discharging violently on the Israel–Palestine conflict had, to borrow Royal Holloway's term, made antisemitism 'a potentially sensitive topic' for the classroom. More so with the current turmoil about the issue of antisemitism in the recently Corbyn-led Labour Party.

Royal Holloway also has an active Jewish student society and sizeable enrolment. More to the point, Royal Holloway set up, in 2000, the 'Holocaust Research Centre'. It proudly declares itself the British university leader in this field as an 'international, interdisciplinary forum, bringing together researchers working on different aspects of the Holocaust in areas including history, literary and language studies, film and media studies, philosophy and sociology'.

It marks, as a university, not departmental, event, a Holocaust Memorial Day every January and a distinguished speaker is invited to lecture. Royal Holloway is the only university in the UK to run an MA course solely dedicated to the field of Holocaust studies. It stands in the university course catalogue alongside the above MA course in English studies.

Return with all this in mind to Dickens's *Oliver Twist*. The story ('Please, sir, I want some more' etc.) is now, with twenty or more film and TV versions, folkloric. Having run away from Mudfog (probably Rochester), as an abused orphanage child and juvenile chimney sweep, Oliver finds himself starving and exhausted on the outskirts of London.

He is befriended (actually recruited) by the 'Artful Dodger', a juvenile delinquent of cockney charm, Jack Dawkins, who gives Oliver some tucker and offers him a place to sleep. The Dodger then conducts Oliver through to a criminal quarter of London, around present-day Clerkenwell. Dickens describes it double-bore blast:

> The sole places that seemed to prosper amid the general blight of the place, were the public-houses; and in them, the lowest orders of Irish were wrangling with might and main. Covered ways and yards, which here and there diverged from the main street, disclosed little knots of houses, where drunken men and women were positively wallowing in filth; and from several of the door-ways, great ill-looking fellows were cautiously emerging, bound, to all appearance, on no very well-disposed or harmless errands.

Dickens's novel is, incidentally, set in his own 1837 present day, a 'novel with a purpose'. Its purpose was to attack the 1834 Poor Law Amendment whose policy was to make the workhouses so cruel they would force able-bodied paupers back to work ('austerity' *avant la lettre*). It was not, in Boz's opinion, the answer. Neither, Dickens believed, was driving the poor to crime as their sole 'rational choice'.

Finally, the two lads reach their destination: 'a dirty and more wretched place [Oliver] had never seen. The street was very narrow and muddy, and the air was impregnated with filthy odours.'

After some apparently necessary shibboleths, Oliver finds himself inside a house. Going up a broken staircase, the Dodger takes him into a large upper room:

The walls and ceiling of the room were perfectly black with age and dirt. There was a deal table before the fire: upon which were a candle, stuck in a ginger-beer bottle, two or three pewter pots, a loaf and butter, and a plate. In a frying-pan, which was on the fire, and which was secured to the mantelshelf by a string, some sausages were cooking; and standing over them, with a toasting-fork in his hand, was a very old shrivelled Jew, whose villainous-looking and repulsive face was obscured by a quantity of matted red hair. He was dressed in a greasy flannel gown, with his throat bare; and seemed to be dividing his attention between the frying-pan and the clothes-horse, over which a great number of silk handkerchiefs were hanging. Several rough beds made of old sacks, were huddled side by side on the floor. Seated round the table were four or five boys, none older than the Dodger, smoking long clay pipes, and drinking spirits with the air of middle-aged men. These all crowded about their associate as he whispered a few words to the Jew; and then turned round and grinned at Oliver. So did the Jew himself, toasting-fork in hand. 'This is him, Fagin,' said Jack Dawkins; 'my friend Oliver Twist.'

The handkerchiefs, stolen by Fagin's trained child pickpockets ('county line' juvenile criminals *avant la lettre*), are being de-snotted for resale. It adds little relish to the bangers.

A number of things stand out. 'Sausages', primarily – one can almost smell them: they are pork, of course. Non-kosher. One might argue that Dickens wants to make the point that Fagin is a bad Jew – not at all like those lads he saw every day around University College. Or, one might argue, he is indulging in *Der Stürmer*-style racist caricature.

The trident fork and the red hair are symbolic in racist depictions of Jews and, connectedly, folk depictions of the devil. Satan and Judas (his agent) are assumed to be 'gingers'. One can quibble. If Fagin is an 'old shrivelled Jew', his hair would be grey, not as Dickens describes it, matted red. Stage Shylocks, incidentally, routinely wore red wigs until the twentieth century.[*]

In popular cartoon depiction, Satan carries a three-pronged fork the better to torment his subjects, roasting and prodding them, as Fagin does his sausages, in Hell. For eternity. The word 'Jew' occurs a superfluous three times in the passage. It occurs 260 times, always referring to Fagin, in the following

---

[*]   It was plausibly a folk memory of this that led Diane Abbott to declare antisemitism as a prejudice equivalent to that against red heads in her letter to *The Observer* in April 2023.

twenty chapters before Dickens realised he was overdoing it and went easy on the word. But not the image. Fagin slithering through the night-time East End streets late in the novel – to arrange the murder of Nancy – is shudderingly described as being 'like some loathsome reptile, engendered in the slime and darkness'. A golem, the mythic Jewish monster made of mud and excrement.

One can pile up evidence that Dickens's depiction of Fagin is grossly antisemitic and, worse still, knowledgeable about anti-semitic mythology (red hair, forks, etc.) with a willingness to make use of it. Whether Dickens himself, over the long course of his life, was antisemitic is a moot point. The evidence is that he may not have entirely been.[*] But after the Indian Uprising in 1857 (see above), it is incontrovertible that his racism discharged even more harshly elsewhere. It was in him, always looking for some target to discharge on.

As regards Royal Holloway's triggering, suppose, as a mind game, in the Victorian culture course the seminar on *Oliver Twist* were held in the same week as the university's, and the world's, Holocaust Memorial Day in January. What would the campus reverberations be? What would the conversation be in the student union?

I commend the bravery of Royal Holloway's Victorian culture course designers for not taking the easy way out with, say, Dickens's novel about factory strikes and capitalism, *Hard Times*. They chose a thornier text, particularly on their

---

[*] See the sympathetically portrayed character Riah in his last complete novel, *Our Mutual Friend*.

campus. I would like to have been a fly on the wall at the *Oliver Twist* seminar. Royal Holloway's choosing and triggering it is five-star correct. I only wish they hadn't been so vague defending the rightness of what they were doing.

THE OLD TESTAMENT: TOO HOT TO HANDLE

In late February 2022, it became known that Newman University, a theological institution in Birmingham, had triggered the Second Book of Samuel for its undergraduate classes. The apparently strange warning was 'exposed' via the indefatigably resourceful Chris Hastings in the *Mail on Sunday*. Headlines pointed out that the university was named 'after Cardinal John Henry Newman' (i.e. it was of Catholic foundation).

The reasons given by the university were 'sexual violence and abuse'. In effect, they were giving an episode of the Old Testament a quadruple 'X', hot sex, rating. It was not, apparently, the first part of the book of books which had come under their trigger. The university's curricular committee had devised an acronym for sections deemed trigger worthy. In this case, it was 'SV'. Whether to deter, alert or suggest skipping was not clear.

While acknowledging it believed a warning was necessary, the university insisted it was casting no aspersion on the Bible as the Word of God. Or any suggestion the books of Samuel be relegated to the Apocrypha.

More narrative background than the *Mail on Sunday* had space for is required. David, the third King of Israel, is given, in the two books of Samuel, the longest, most complete, life history of any character in the Bible: more completely detailed even than his descendant Jesus's Rashomon-like four-life stories in the New Testament.

To summarise the prelude to the SV episode: the historical date, theologians calculate, is around 1,000 BC. That point at which history meets oral legend. The young David begins life a poor shepherd boy, the son of Jesse of Bethlehem. He has in addition to his crook a slingshot to protect his flock against lions (roaming at this period in the Middle East) and wolves.

The Prophet Samuel declares, after a vision, that this humble lad is the future of Israel. God's chosen. The current king, Saul, to eliminate this potential rival and avoid a bloody battle with the Philistines (Palestinians), allows the boy, with only his slingshot as armament, to fight for Israel, as its champion, against the gigantically invincible Philistine champion, Goliath. A mistake. David fells his foe with a pebble. David will, over the course of his seventy-year life, smite many Philistines on the hip.

He grows up a mighty warrior in the increasingly paranoid Saul's service. He has an explicitly gay relationship with Saul's son Jonathan: 'very pleasant hast thou been unto me', he says after his beloved dies in battle, 'thy love to me was wonderful, passing the love of women'.

Out of self-interest, not love, he marries, with a purchase price of 100 Philistine foreskins, one of King Saul's many daughters, Michal. He is now seen as an even more likely rival for the throne and exiled. The exiler Saul is slain in battle.

David assumes power, defeating, in civil war, Saul's lineal claimants, led by Ish-bosheth. A name which, unlike David, Saul and Jonathan, has never been popular at the Christian font.

David tacitly arranges for his rival to be assassinated. He then executes the assassins, removing their hands and feet – lest anyone think of doing to him what he has had done to the son of Saul, formerly heir apparent.

David's personal prophet, Nathan – who receives visionary communication from Moses and the Almighty Himself – confirms David's assumption as Jehovah's will for Israel. David's ruthlessness, treachery and usurpation is exculpated by divine absolution. No punishment is forthcoming. Yet.

King David is now thirty and has had, we are casually informed, six wives, six sons by them and uncounted concubines. He is now, after Jonathan, athletically heterosexual. To become a nation, Israel needs to be fruitful and multiply beyond its tribal numbers. There is no shame in his spreading his seed far and wide, any more than there was in his relationship with Jonathan. Sexual promiscuity strengthens Israel at this critical moment in its history.

David's early union with Michal has merged royal lines and he reigns over a unified Israel. But weakness of the flesh, the biblical narrative suggests, is a danger to him. Or is it? God moves in mysterious ways. It is the Almighty's current interest, one is led to believe, not to pass individual judgement on righteous or unrighteous sons of Israel but to progress Israel from tribe to people to nation.

The proto-nation is still embattled. King David does not make Saul's mistake of taking to the field himself with the risk of leaving the throne empty and the country directionless should he be killed or usurped while away. He masterminds strategy from his HQ in Jerusalem, keeping the home front strong.

Israel is currently besieging the heathen Ammonite town of Rabbah. One of David's paladins, comprising Israel's thirty-seven mightiest warriors, is Uriah the Hittite (a convert to Judaism from an insignificant tribe). He is known but not a comrade of his monarch to whom he is utterly devoted. That he is a favourite is evident from his having a luxurious home viewably next to David's Jerusalem castle.

There follows the triggerable 'SV' episode for Cardinal Newman pupils, Birmingham AD 2022.

From his castle roof in Jerusalem, taking the evening air, David sees, in an adjoining building, a beautiful naked woman bathing herself. Whether in twilight or by candlelight is not said. Uriah, her husband as it transpires, is currently at the front doing battle for David at Rabbah.

Bathsheba's ablution is not, in the Bible, overtly voluptuous – although writers and artists through the ages (notably Rembrandt) have assumed it was. She is cleansing herself, according to religious rite, seven days after her menstrual cycle.

She is, thus, 'pure' and fertile. David enquires and is told she is Bathsheba, Uriah's recently married wife, a currently child-less woman of noble descent. He instructs his guard to 'take' and bring her to him. They have sex. Whether it is voluntary, passively accepted or forced is not clear. That it is wrong is crystal clear. Bathsheba is sent home directly after. David feels guilt and must fear God's anger in the person of Nathan.

Given the personnel involved, and castle gossip, everyone knows what he and Bathsheba have done. Except Uriah. Bathsheba was ovulating on the night David 'took' her and reports to him she is pregnant. Uriah returns a hero from the still continuing battle. David has summoned him and welcomes him, ostensibly for his military exploits, and tells him to go home and be welcomed, in bed, by his wife – whom he pretends not to know. He has earned some R&R. He plies him with drink. Uriah, however, refuses to rest in his marital bed – sexual intercourse will weaken his prowess: his men at the front have no housing. He sleeps rough outside David's castle gates before returning to Rabbah to slaughter more Ammonites for Israel. He deserves a medal, not the cuckold's horns.

David's sneaky plan – that Uriah will unknowingly 'father' his king's child – is foiled. He makes another more dastardly plan. He writes a letter to Joab, the supreme military commander at Rabbah, instructing that Uriah be posted in the van (as point man) in the fighting and his fellow warriors' retreat, leaving him alone to be 'smitten'. Murdered, that is. Uriah himself delivers the sealed letter, his death warrant, to Joab: a gratuitous touch.

Uriah is duly smitten. David is in the clear – the cover up will be that Bathsheba is carrying Uriah's child. But David has reckoned without Nathan, who has one ear to the ground, the other to heaven. He comes and poses a parable. It reverts to

David's childhood. There are two shepherds: one is immense-ly rich with a huge flock; the other has but one lamb. The rich shepherd steals the poor shepherd's lamb. What should happen to the thief, Nathan asks the king?

'Kill him,' David answers. 'Thou art the man!' retorts Nathan. He then delivers God's judgement. David and Bathsheba will survive. Their illegitimate child will not. To protect Bathsheba from being stoned as an adulteress, the couple marry. Their baby boy dies as prophesied. Another is engendered; he is Sol-omon: destined to be a king of unified Israel.

After Nathan's denunciation, David pulls himself back to-gether. It is not said whether Bathsheba ever knows of David's homicidal disposal of her first husband. Younger by decades than David, she grows old to become a behind-the-scenes kingmaker, scheming to ensure Solomon succeeds David, not one of his other claimant sons. The resourceful Bathsheba is listed in the New Testament as one of the ancestresses of Jesus. From sexual victim she becomes, over the years, a woman of power. A question hovers over the whole episode: was it all from the first part of God's design?

The other hovering question is what posterity is to make of this white-hot melodrama? As summarised, it is Danielle Steel with a strong dash of film noir. It does not, on the face of it, seem in key with the Old Testament. It seems, in fact, more at home, three millennia on, on the fictional page and cinema screen.

In 1951, the hit movie of the year was the spectacular big screen 'epic' *David and Bathsheba*. There was geopolitical background. In 1948, the state of Israel had been created. It confirmed its existence with a victorious war of defence against biblical Arab foes. It was, after revelations of the horrors of the Nazi death camps, Exodus for what remained of European Jewry.

Hollywood, with its American Jewish power elite at studio level, American Jewish genius at directorial levels and American Jewish talent at player level, celebrated the creation of Israel with two spectacular, and spectacularly successful, Technicolor epics celebrating Old Testament heroes. The first, in 1949, was *Samson and Delilah* – Victor Mature playing him, Hedy Lamarr her.

Two years later, in 1951, came *David and Bathsheba*, Gregory Peck playing him, Susan Hayward her. Peck, yet to take on Atticus Finch, was the embodiment of gentile American, manly decencies: Catholic by upbringing. David, if one follows the account in Samuel, is a low-down dirty, no-good two-timer (to borrow Hollywood parlance). Not at first sight a role for Gregory Peck. The script and screenplay were by Philip Dunne, a highly skilled, Catholic by upbringing, writer.

A preface informs the audience that the narrative is based on the Second Book of Samuel. But the Biblical/Torah story, while retaining the source's outline, is reframed for present-day Hollywood and Eisenhower America. The film is free on YouTube and repays watching. It has the flavour of the time and place of its making and Hollywood skill in handling sometimes awkward material.

Bathsheba is portrayed by Hayward as a smarter Delilah.

Money is not her aim: power is what she wants. She deliber-
ately flaunts herself in the bath scene, aware that David (whose
marriage with Michal is breaking up) is watching. She throws
herself into an affair. She, not he, is the sexual predator. A
dominant flavouring in the late '40s and early '50s Hollywood
films was femmes fatales – Delilahs.

Higher educational institutions are run by smart people.
Why, then, did the Newman University trigger this particular
biblical episode? For two reasons evidently. It raises complex
theological questions about the Old Testament Jehovah and
the temporal world. Has He, the Almighty, changed His mind
about what humanity needs by the time of the New Testament
gospels? Secondly, the triggering is, one suspects, a cheese on
the mousetrap ruse: to make the students curious, read deeply
and think hard. Hot scenes make for lively seminars. I would
like to have attended these.

YOUTH'S CRUEL TRIGGER

Dr Becky Albertalli had made her first career as a psychologist
'specializing in gender nonconforming children and LGBTQ
teens and adults.'* The work meant one-on-one intimate communication with the young. And a quiveringly high degree of
empathetic 'sensitivity'.

'Young adult' ('YA') fiction has been one of the phenomenal
areas of growth in the late twentieth- and early 21st-century

---

* For further information on Becky Albertalli and her bruising experience of YA, web-based
  'sensitivity' reading, see Katy Waldman, 'Is My Novel Offensive?', *Slate* (8 February 2017).

book trade. As a genre, it speaks to teens: often offering, wrapped in fiction, soft therapy of the 'you are not alone now' kind. Teens speak back to their genre, and about it, on the web. Voluminously. The genre has volcanic energy: it is heated and eruptive. Anyone writing YA fiction will find themselves in a triangular relationship with publisher, reader and – more significantly – choric web reaction.

Demographically, the author, who has spent years perfecting their craft, may well find themselves writing across a divide of years to readerships younger than themselves. J. D. Salinger finished writing *The Catcher in the Rye* (1951) aged thirty-one: was he really 'into' the teenage Holden Caulfield living in the 1950s present day? Is that much-revered novel 'authentic'?

Becky Albertalli resolved in her thirties to extend her communication with young adult teens into YA fiction. Teens, that is, adjusting themselves to the rest of their lives. If she wrote skilfully enough, she hoped, she could bring a wealth of professionally acquired expertise to not one at a time but millions (as it eventually turned out). It was a 'reaching over' exercise. She had done it routinely as a therapist treating troubled teens.

Becky Albertalli was born in 1982. She is married and a mother of two and, when she published her first novel, owner of a dog, Bieber, who breaks into her first narrative. Her agent found her the top publisher, HarperCollins, with a strong subsidiary list of YA titles. Her first book, aged thirty-three, was published in 2015. *Simon vs. the Homo Sapiens Agenda*. 'Homo' was the hook in the title.

It is, as reviewers of the author's age and older agreed, a fine novel. 'Steal this [book] from your teen,' Oprah's magazine advised. It was made from that moment. The story is ingeniously constructed. Simon Spier is an everyday seventeen-year-old schoolboy living in 'Shady Creek', Georgia, backwoods deep south. He knows he is gay. No one else knows. He has erotic dreams about Harry Potter whom, he believes, he resembles as played by the teenage Daniel Radcliffe.

Accidentally, Simon comes across, on the web, someone in the same predicament as himself: a covert young gay individual. They give each other *noms de gmail*, 'Jacques' (Simon, the narrator) and 'Blue' (the unknown other). Email is their confessional; they are each other's priest. Or, more relevantly, each other's lay psychotherapist. Shrouded in secrecy, they come to know each other intimately, without knowing each other by face or Facebook. Albertalli handles this technique expertly.

The plot is slight. Simon's email is hacked. He is first black-mailed then brutally outed on Tumblr: the least private of e-communication channels. But, to his amazement, he finds sympathy from his friends, family, schoolmates (on the whole) and schoolteachers. He had nothing to fear. The surprise of finding out who Blue was is well managed. The novel ends with a kiss, not sex.

The novel breathes cosy reassurance. There are discussions about race, but (even in Georgia!) prejudice is now history. Blue is patrilinear American Jewish, it emerges; Simon's best female friend, Abby Suso, is African American but 'so what?' Simon and his seventeen-year-old best friends drive to school.

One of them is mocked, in a best-friendly way, for having a 'Flintstones-era car'.

The world of the novel is one without poor people, sexual perverts, racial prejudice or far-right politics. There is only the *Sturm und Drang* of adolescence with, as Simon discovers, safety nets all the way. Suicide? Never heard of it. Simon's Shady Creek is not Molly Russell's *Riverdale*. Which is the truer?

Author, publisher, agent were happy as pie with Albertalli's debut work. The reading public and prize-awarding bodies were even happier. As Wikipedia (whose coverage of YA fiction is knowledgeable) records:

> Albertalli received the William C. Morris Award from the American Library Association, an annual honor for young adult literature, as well as internationally the German Youth Literature Prize. The novel was also featured on the National Book Award Longlist and listed by the *Wall Street Journal* as one of the Best Young Adult novels in 2015.

Albertalli's novel was adapted into a film, *Love, Simon* (2018), which made a ton of money – five times its production costs.

What more could a young(ish) writer expect from her breakthrough novel? But to her astonishment, Albertalli received stringent online denunciation from her YA readership for her offensive 'fetishization of queer girls'. Another question came at her from all angles: 'why is Simon gay? Why did you, a cishet woman, write a book about a gay teen boy?' Bluntly, what right had Mrs Becky Albertalli to write this book? The question was not asked politely. Basically, the implication was that she had offended the #OwnVoices authenticity criterion and must pay for it.

Her 'advanced' age was a recurrent target. She could have replied she was about the same age as J. K. Rowling when the first *Harry Potter* was published (and Harry is Simon's god). But Rowling was, in 2015, becoming contentious. Gibed at also was Albertalli's command of 21st-century teen argot. Every adolescent generation remodulates its private language and Albertalli's idiom was struggling to catch up – adequately for the adult ear but not for youth of the moment.

Albertalli declared herself 'crushed'. She had been cancelled by a key segment of her aimed-at readership. 'You really don't *know* what it is to be us' was the charge. How to fend it off? By 'feelers', not the psychotherapist's remote 'objectivity', was, she decided, the answer.

Becky Albertalli's second young-adult novel, *The Upside of Unrequited* (2017), was submitted in prepublication, still wet-clay form, to a jury-sized dozen 'sensitivity readers', some in-house, some freelance, to assert or advise necessary changes. The 'readers', like those aimed at, belonged to the YA cohort; those for whom 'f/f', 'mlm' and '#OwnVoices' were everyday usage.

Albertalli herself was now in sight of forty. Potential reader-bruising areas of her first draft included 'LGBTQ, black, Korean American, anxiety, obesity, and Jewish representation issues, among others'. A boxful of eggshells for the author to walk over, but now she had assistance. Radical revision happened. The traditional editorial function had been diffused to a readers' group (not highly paid – according to *Slate*, freelance sensitivity readers get an average $250 per manuscript).

Albertalli's commercial success continued to soar and her problems with it. The YA assault continued even more savagely. Newspaper and online profiles, particularly with the success of the film of her first novel, *Love, Simon*, identified her as a married mother, who had surrendered her ethnically identifying original surname, 'Goldstein', whose own young adult years were two decades gone.

The problem with her follow-up girl-on-girl novel, *Leah on the Offbeat* (2018), became even sharper, coinciding within a month as it did with the release of the film *Love, Simon*, to huge acclaim.

This is Goodreads' capsule summary: 'Leah Burke – girl-band drummer, master of deadpan, and Simon Spier's best friend from the award-winning *Simon vs. the Homo Sapiens Agenda* – takes center stage in this novel of first love and senior-year angst.'

The source of her angst is that she's bi and finds it out awkwardly. Goodreads, incidentally, gave the novel its 'Best Young Adult Novel of 2018' award.

This novel broke new ground for Albertalli: 'It was my first time writing a love story between two girls – actually, it was my first time writing from the perspective of a character who's attracted to girls.'

Like its predecessors, it went straight into the *New York Times* bestseller list. Nonetheless, Albertalli was again subjected to downright abuse from the YA community online for whom the Old Gray Lady was just that. It was, she said, 'often searingly personal. I was frequently mentioned by name, held up again and again as the quintessential example of allocishet* inauthenticity. I was a straight woman writing shitty queer books for the straights, profiting off of communities I had no connection to.'

She exploded into riposte: 'I'm thirty-seven years old. I've been happily married to a guy for almost ten years. I have two kids and a cat. I've never kissed a girl. I never even realized I wanted to.'

In the neologism 'an allocishet woman', she had been accused of writing from the alien standpoint of post-YA age and – in the context – deviant 'straightness'.

'But,' Albertalli declared, 'if I rewind further, I'm pretty sure I've had crushes on boys and girls for most of my life. I just didn't realize the girl crushes were crushes.'

It's not much of a defence: 'I did it, but I didn't know I was doing it.' But she was clearly out of ammunition. Becky Albertalli, judged by her own testimony, came close to psychic breakdown as an author. Was this what it was to be one of the most successful fiction writers of your day?

---

* As the website Urban Dictionary defines 'allocishet': 'Someone who is allosexual & alloromantic (completely experiences sexual & romantic attraction), heterosexual (is attracted solely to members of the opposite gender) and is cisgender (someone whose sex is their biological gender).'

You know what's a mindfuck? Questioning your sexual identity in your thirties when every self-appointed literary expert on Twitter has to share their hot take on the matter … Imagine if you had a Greek chorus of internet strangers propping up your imposter syndrome at every stage of the process … Even as I write this, I'm bracing for the inevitable discourse – I could draft the twitter threads myself if I wanted to … But if I can ask for something, it's this: will you sit for a minute with the discomfort of knowing you may have been wrong about me?

A forlorn hope, one fears. Literary success can be a bitter fruit.

HUCK FINN: GOOD NOVEL, BAD WORD

The Adventures of Huckleberry Finn was triggered by the University of Exeter at the start of the 2022 academic year. A conscientious university American literature course could hardly duck Mark Twain's novel in the light of Ernest Hemingway's encomium: 'It's the best book we've had. All American writing comes from that. There was nothing before.'

Huckleberry Finn the novel did not have an easy relationship with America for many years. It was for decades boycotted by libraries and schools. The reason is evident from the first sentence: 'You don't know about me, without you have read a book by the name of *The Adventures of Tom Sawyer*, but that ain't no matter.'

The novel sanctioned bad grammar and – in the little outlaw

Huck's regard for the world's rules – 'sass' (i.e. cheek). What Hemingway admired is that you can *hear* Huck: his voice rises from the page. And what you hear is an echt American voice – forget the slang.

What renders the novel triggerable again, 140 years after its publication, is Huck's 219 uses of just one word. There are no easy ways round it. There are uneasy ways. Alan Gribben, a professor at Auburn University, published in 2011 an edition in which all usages of the offending word were replaced by 'slave'. Otherwise, the text was pristine. But maimed. To 'correct' Huck's regional dialect is to geld the book: it is as if the opening sentence had read: 'You won't, dear reader, have the faintest idea who I am unless you happen to have already read *The Adventures of Tom Sawyer*. But that really is of not the slightest importance to what I shall tell you.'

Huckleberry Finn the novel, as given to us by Mark Twain, is as unmendable as its eponymous hero. Its 'American grain', to borrow William Carlos Williams's term, resists being anything but what it is. The University of Exeter's English department hedged their bets by triggering *Huck Finn* on the grounds that its depiction of the African American runaway slave 'Jim' (being a slave he has no surname: that would suggest his having a past as a human being) was 'problematic in a number of ways'. Indeed.

The department's trigger is, in my view, commendable in that – without 'leading' or 'closing' argument – it opens up the novel for discussion on a number of fronts. It alerts the reader. What problems? The trigger opens the novel for students of colour (there will in 2022 be more than in 1982) to interrogate the text with BLM in mind.

One problem is dates. Twain's novel was published in 1884 but set in the 1830s, when black slavery (as common in the north as in the south) was a majority-approved, or at least accepted, fact of American life. Abolitionism anywhere in the country was nugatory. History records that slavery was overthrown in the late 1860s by the Civil War. But, Twain asks, was it really? Was it entirely? Where and what is the sixty-year-old Jim now as the century draws to an end? Did he get his forty acres and a mule? 'Free, free, free at last!' Or perhaps not. The novel seems not to care.

Another problem worth investigating (although few commentators, as I observe, have done so) is that unlike Tom Sawyer (an Anglo-Saxon surname), Huck is Irish American (Finn is a common Irish name).[*]

The American Irish population, particularly after their mass immigration to the US during the 1840s famine years, were an ethnic group ('Micks') despised and feared after the 1860s – a main theme in Martin Scorsese's movie *Gangs of New York* (2002).

A further discussable problem in the narrative is that, as they float on their raft, Jim becomes Huck's Man Friday – his servant. It's pull that rope, tote that bale for Jim again – Huck's galley slave.

Most troublingly, perhaps, is that Jim is abusive as a father

---

[*]   See Anthony Trollope's 1867 novel, *Phineas Finn: The Irish Member*.

and negligent as a husband. He slaps, violently, his deaf and mute daughter. He deserts her and his wife to save himself. He, of course, has no option. At the end, he is freed (by manumission not Abraham Lincoln), but he (or Twain, as maker of the novel's plot) seems to be uninterested in him rejoining his family (are they also free?) as husband and father.

Twain has bequeathed us, as Exeter's triggering warns, a highly problematic novel – something that need not diminish its literary standing but must be taken on board by serious readers. Exeter University's literature department's act of triggering – read with suspicious care – is surely justified. The seminar's attendees should be on highest alert, their minds maximally open.

OTHERBOUND OTHERPAIN

'Autism has opened worlds to me,' declared the author of *Otherbound*, Corinne Duyvis.* It's a YA sci-fi novel, marketed for thirteen- to seventeen-year-olds. The parents' advisory site Common Sense Media had harsh things to say:

> Parents need to know that *Otherbound* is chock-full of violence. Although the violence takes place in a fantasy realm called the Dunelands, it bears a striking resemblance to the ongoing issues in the Middle East. The main character Amara is a teenage servant whose earliest memory is of her

---

* For more on Duyvis and her innovative OwnVoices genre, see pp. 47–9.

tongue being cut out. Servant women from the Dunelands don't need their tongues because they're not meant to be heard. Amara is frequently beaten by her male captor, and at one point her nose is broken from being slammed into a porcelain bowl. One man is killed in a fistfight, and a magic curse causes the natural world to attack Amara if she attempts to escape. Teens engage in consensual sexual relationships, and two girls share a passionate kiss. LGBTQ themes are explored.

Red flags flutter.

Otherbound is unholed by parental fusillades like the above. It is a significant work of feminist-juvenile sci-fi. It has clear tributes to Frank Herbert's *Dune* and, more distantly, Shakespeare's *Romeo and Juliet*. Its narrative time-shifts record an authorial debt to Octavia E. Butler's *Kindred*.*

Otherbound's plot is convoluted. Seventeen-year-old Nolan Santiago is, to the outside eye, just another schoolkid in a small Arizona town – a hot, desert-like state. He's a failing, friendless, pupil. Totally distracted. Autism? No, the diagnosis from know-nothing physicians is 'virtually constant epilepsy'. He lives with fits. During one of the more protracted walking blackouts, he was hit by a truck and lost a foot.

The truth is every time he blinks Nolan's no longer in Arizona but cross-dimensionally in the mind of a young girl on Dunelands. She, Amara, is unaware of the worm, Nolan, in her

---

* For *Kindred*, see pp. 186–8.

head. Amara's life is as adventurous as brain parasite Nolan's is dull. She is a servant assigned to the renegade princess Cilla, who has been cursed and is in constant flight. Amara's tongue was ripped out at birth (she is a servant, brutally abused by her master, Jorn). She 'signs'. She is, nonetheless, a powerful mage and protects the princess (with whom her relationship may be romantic) by deflecting supernaturally generated physical attacks onto herself. She does so by smearing Cilla's blood on her body. She protects herself by unconsciously transferring the pain to Nolan, her whipping boy. Amara's master – realising she can withstand torment – cuts and burns her for his sadistic gratification. She cannot scream and lives in a world of other-harm.

All the MCs (main characters) are people of colour. The novel juxtaposes two worlds: the mundane and the fantastic. The portal, and passport, is pain. The narrative is suffused with suffering. A new medication given to Nolan renders him known to Amara and an agent, no longer merely a passively suffering observer. He and Amara ally themselves in protection of Cilla, who turns out to be something more than what she seemed.

Generically, *Otherbound* is fantasy. But is it Nolan's fantasy? The escapism of a disabled youth whose only consolation is imagination? Is Dunelands a fantasised Arizona (a state half of which is desert – famously home to the Yuma Imperial Sand Dunes)? Is Nolan simply epileptic? A disorder known, in Greek mythology, as the 'sacred disease'.

How should a parent warned via Common Sense Media who takes the trouble to read the novel address the book with their thirteen-to-seventeen-year-old who has it in their school satchel? Or, more likely, on their 'device'? A very modern dilemma. And, perhaps, none of the parents' bloody business.

UNCONSENTING SLEEPING BEAUTIES

In early March 2023, the national press, led by the *Sunday Telegraph*, reported that Ladybird Books (now owned by Penguin) had hired 'sensitivity' and 'inclusivity' readers to review their catalogue of fairytales for 'offensive content'.

Not, one deduced, content offensive to children but their elders. Ladybird kept its cards close to its chest having learned from the Roald Dahl brouhaha not to kick the hornet's nest where children's literature was concerned. Nonetheless, some facts about revisions to *Cinderella* and *Sleeping Beauty* leaked. The *Mail* pounced: 'Now Ladybird's fairytales get the "sensitivity reader" treatment! Classics like *Cinderella* and *Sleeping Beauty* to be re-examined after being branded "outdated or harmful" for lack of "inclusivity" and "problematic tropes".'

Most problematic, it seemed, was a 'lack of diversity among blonde-haired and blue-eyed protagonists'. Other 'offensive' (i.e. hallowed by tradition) tropes were 'ageism and presumptions of gender pronouns'. No more hallowing.

Five thousand miles away, in Anaheim, California, Disneyland – whose business was fairy stories – was undergoing similar throes. Disney had begun as a studio in the early days of film as a short-break cartoon maker – famously with 'Mickey Mouse'. The studio's first full-length feature movie – *Snow White and the Seven Dwarfs* – came out, in colour, in 1937. It represented a huge leap forward in film technology. It had a full sequential narrative, not merely, like the newspaper 'funnies', comic situations and formulaic cartoon character.

The film is largely unshowable today for its discriminatory depiction of size-challenged humans as clowns (especial-ly 'Dopey') and its 'Prince Charming' presumptions about romance and the passive maiden ('some day my prince will come'). The stress on 'white' and the mother–daughter compe-tition for 'who is the *fairest* in the land' are out of kilter with the 2020s. Snow White has no name – her identity is her whiter than white skin and cherry lips: nothing else (Disney was deli-cate about her upper body – but it is youth semi-pin-up style). The queen's portrayal as a part-time witch has antisemitic characterisation. Most discomfiting, for its necrophiliac-rape implications, is the prince's kiss, which brings Snow White's necessarily non-compliant cadaver back to life.

The same invasive male-on-unconsenting-female kiss (with the same reanimating effect) is thematically central in Disney's *Sleeping Beauty* (1959). Like the Snow White fable, it is sourced from Charles Perrault's 1697 collection of fairy tales – Disney's motherlode.

A 'Snow White and Her Adventures' dark ride (i.e. in the dark) featured in the 'Fantasyland' division of the Anaheim

Disneyland when it opened in 1955. The park has, since then, become one of America's genuinely universal experiences. As it was calculated in November 2022: 'Overall, 87 per cent of Americans have been to a theme park or amusement park. Of this group, 74 per cent have visited a Disney park. Baby boomers ages 57 to 76 are the most likely generation to have been to a Disney park.'

Disney is, like it or not, embedded into the American sensibility.

The Snow White ride is one of the few which has survived to the present day in Disney's now multifarious theme park iterations in Florida, Tokyo and Paris. In 1983, it went gothic as 'Snow White's Scary Adventures'. Anaheim took advantage of the Covid shutdowns to revamp the ride again, at a cost of half a million dollars. It would be retitled 'Snow White's Enchanted Wish' with a new inflection.

Disney has three core categories of consumer: adult; adolescent; boys and girls. This new 'Enchanted Wish' manifestation would aim at all three but with a stress on the young female visitor. The 'dwarfs' were not now adult males but lovable toddlers. No Dopey. Snow White was recreated as a kind of resourceful adoptive mother figure or elder sibling.

It was still a dark ride. But Disney's 'Imagineers' had created 'animatronic' (with occasional 'smell' experience) scenes, loosely based on acceptable parts of the 1937 film narrative. The new ride opened on 30 April 2021 to an approving review from the *Los Angeles Times* and other publications knowledgeable about the theme park industry which, like the movie industry, California had given to the world. Kids, reportedly, loved the refurbished Snow White.*

There emerged, however, a slower developing wave of criticism about this new jewel in the Disney crown. The unconsenting kiss was at its centre. Emma Hatheway voiced what became a widespread objection to Disney's 'sleeping beauty' motif, AD 2021:

> Beyond the damaging portrayal of women as domesticated creatures and the exaggeration of their physical appearances, there are also indisputable references and allusions to rape and sexual assault in the Disney Princess franchise. The overall permeating storyline of the knight in shining armour that is the princess' saviour 'denies women the agency' or any ability to make her own decisions. This is exhibited in the way the men dominate the screen and the female characters, leading to issues of power, control and mastery that are rooted in rape culture. Taking away a woman's authority and sense of self by allowing men to dominate them sexually and emotionally is extremely dangerous for young children to view and digest as a form of entertainment.

Will this last iteration of Perrault via Uncle Walt survive? As things now look, probably not. But Disney, the nearest thing

---

* I have been on the first two; not yet the third.

to America's established religion, will for as long as the Philadelphia Liberty Bell rings.

#DVPIT

Acronymically and symbolically, '#DVpit' stands for 'diverse voices, twitter pitch event'. How it works is explained on its website (their stress):

> #DVpit is a pitch event created to showcase *pitches from unagented, marginalized voices that have been historically underrepresented in publishing.* This may include (but is not limited to): Black, Indigenous, People of Color (BIPOC); people living and/or born/raised in marginalized cultures and countries; disabled persons (includes neurodivergence and mental illness); people on marginalized ends of the cultural and/or religious spectrum; people identifying within LGBTQIA+; and more. *Any decisions regarding eligibility are yours to make.* Creators are not obligated to disclose anything they do not feel comfortable with and are not required to pitch only work that reflects their own identity, though that is certainly welcome!
>
> The first #DVpit took place on April 19, 2016 and was a national trending hashtag on Twitter. Since then, there have been hundreds of creators signed by agents and countless book deals contracted as a direct result of this event, with editors from small to mid-size to Big Five publishers requesting to receive the manuscripts at submission stage.

DVpit action takes the form of web-based 'pitch events'. They are one-day dated and twelve-hour timed matching sessions between talent and the book industry. The site has had notable successes: commercially and in centralising the marginal(ised) voice. Some successes, however, fall back into the pit they clambered out of.

In 2018, Amélie Wen Zhao 'matched' with the major commercial publisher Delacorte (a division of Random House) on a DVpit Twitter event. It was a spectacular match with a six-figure book deal offered for a trilogy of YA sci-fi. The next *Hunger Games* was foreseen. Zhao's debut under the Delacorte imprint was scheduled for January 2019.

Zhao, of Chinese heritage, was born in Paris and brought up in Beijing with her grandmother. She immigrated to the US aged eighteen to attend college. She went on to employment in Wall Street, writing fantasy by night. She returns often to China, to relish its legends and landscapes. She can be seen as both marginal and cosmopolitan.

Her first novel, *Blood Heir*, was set in a fantasy setting – the Cyrilian Empire (the name recalls the Russian script, 'Cyrillic' – there are Slavic tinctures throughout). 'Affinites' – who have magical powers – are hated and suppressed.

The emperor's daughter, heiress (by blood) apparent, Anastacya Mikhailov ('Ana' for short) is powerfully Affinite. She can control blood and its circulation in the bodies of others. Her father has kept her in protective seclusion. When he is assassinated, she must hunt down the murderer in order to succeed to the throne. She is aided by wily crime lord Ramson

Quicktongue (English names are not Zhao's forte). The novel is aimed, primarily, at the twelve-to-seventeen-year-old female reader for whom bodily blood can be a sensitive issue.

ARCs (advanced reader copies) distributed to select critics on Twitter and to Goodreads (now affiliated to Amazon) was standard practice to create a YA sales springboard. Zhao's novel did not spring. It was not the plot, or the fantasy setting, but the slavery aspect, particularly a slave auction – which proved contentious. Delacorte advertised the book with the tag 'oppression is blind to skin color'. Early readers had a different view.

It was objected ferociously on social media that Zhao was appropriating and displacing the factuality of centuries-long African American slavery. Ana, and the elite, are golden skinned or tawny – the sheen of Ana's 'dusk gold' complexion is frequently mentioned. The slaves are dark skinned. None of them has MC (main character) status. Twittercrit and Goodreads criticisms with long, demonstrative outtakes of *Blood Heir*'s offensiveness damned the book before, in any commercial sense, it existed.

Zhao was crushed and tweeted saying: 'It was never my intention to bring harm to any reader of this valued community … I have decided to ask my publisher not to publish "Blood Heir" at this time.'

She received approbation from the valued community for still-birthing *Blood Heir*.

Then, after consultation, rereads and revision (for 'incisiveness', it was euphemised), she went ahead. In March 2019,

Blood Heir, and its trilogy, lived once more. The book would be published in November. Zhao laid the way with an open letter:

> In writing this novel, I researched extensively on the subject of modern-day human trafficking and indentured labour throughout the world and specifically from my heritage …
> I hope to share a new perspective from my background as a Chinese immigrant living in America. I am excited for readers to meet my heroine, who believes in justice and is ready to fight for it with her wits, grit, and magic; and for them to have a chance to engage in further dialogue about these important social issues.

The episode indicated a symptomatic grinding of gears between the YA world and the corporate real world. Bluntly, who 'owned' Zhao? The Twitterverse or corporate America and its paying consumers?

How good a novel is *Blood Heir*? As rehashed, it got rave 'reviews' (so-called) on Amazon. Independent web reviewers raved less. It was OK. But no *Hunger Games*. If only YA could find a laureate who wasn't, like Suzanne Collins, sixty years old. Or grey-bearded G. R. R. Martin. The genre keeps looking down into the pit for the real thing.

MISS JULIE: 'PERMANENTLY WITHDRAWN'

In August 2022, an FOI request by *The Times* revealed that Sussex University had 'permanently withdrawn' August

Strindberg's *Miss Julie* (1888) as a taught text and removed it to the dusty Swedish literature section of the university library. The play was judged beyond triggering but not bannable.

The press, led by *The Times*, raised a hue and cry. Scandi noir was well tolerated – viz, Stieg Larsson's *The Girl with the Dragon Tattoo* (2005) – so why not Strindberg? The university replied to *The Times* that two factors were involved. Students taking the undergraduate world literature module in which *Miss Julie* featured had complained about the 'psychological and emotional effects' of Strindberg's drama on them. It was traumatogenic.

Parliament's interest was aroused and Professor Sasha Rose-neil, the vice-chancellor of Sussex University, later explained to the Commons Education Committee which questioned this obliteration of classic literature:

In the context of the Sarah Everard case which had been in the news that year … there was a lot of attention about sexual violence that young women were experiencing [and] a decision was made to swap it for a different text that's equally challenging to students but not around those issues.

There is, in fact, no sexual violence in the play – certainly nothing of the kind that the sordid brute Wayne Couzens inflicted on Sarah Everard. There is in *Miss Julie*, however, quite an extraordinary play with conventional sexuality and its codes. Extraordinary, that is, for its time, 1888.

The plot is set around Midsummer's Eve, the 'white night'

when Scandinavia indulges in an annual Saturnalia. The plot centres on a triangle of socially and emotionally involved characters. Jean – valet to the count in whose house the action takes place – is engaged to a kitchen servant. The count is elsewhere celebrating Midsummer: there is a 'when the cat's away' licence in the house.

The count's daughter, Miss Julie, has recently broken her own engagement when her fiancé refused, in public, to submit himself to a dog-like act of humiliation, involving a whip in her hand. In protest against her class, its restrictions and life itself, Miss Julie throws herself, as a dominatrix, at the estate gamekeeper and Jean. Jean submits – but treacherously. She proposes elopement. He declines. The count returns. Miss Julie is desperate. What can she do? Jean hands her his cut-throat razor. She leaves the stage to use it. Her last act of independence.

The play is well in advance of what British drama was doing until the arrival of George Bernard Shaw in the 1890s, strongly influenced by Ibsen and Strindberg. For the University of Sussex to have 'permanently withdrawn' *Miss Julie* seems an overreaction. But as a spokesperson, earlier than the vice-chancellor, more forthrightly explained: '*Miss Julie* was temporarily removed from one Spring Term module this academic year, due to real concerns over the deep tragedy of recent student suicides.'

Sussex had a student suicide problem, which, to its credit, it was doing all in its power to remedy. It wasn't entirely 'recent'. The university had an active student body and in 2017 its newspaper (*The Tab*) noted, with alarm, that there had been six student and one staff suicides over the past five years. Cry-for-help attempts were not publicly recorded. Suicide is a major cause of premature death for the undergraduate age group. *The Tab* contacted the university for comment. A spokesperson replied: 'It's devastating whenever any person takes their own life ... This is why we take student mental health extremely seriously. While student suicides are thankfully rare, any instance is one too many and we are determined to do everything possible to support all our students through times of difficulty.'

The university had set up a Student Life Centre with staff trained in suicide intervention: available twenty-four hours a day to help students in crisis. Its slogan was 'Students must never feel alone'. But students did.

It was apparent that Sussex was suffering from what sociologists call 'lonely crowd syndrome'. It was not ever so. Sussex was one of the so-called new universities which were set up in the 1960s following the Robbins Report. The report's basic assertion was that higher education was a right for the many, not a privilege for the few.

Sussex, with much publicity, established itself as an institution with the collegiality of Oxbridge – small group and tutorial teaching – along with 'new maps of learning'. The institution has a glamorous aura and at its outset was hugely successful. Success led to more students, dilution and a loss of the organic, interdisciplinary, ideal on which Sussex was founded. A friend of mine, and senior academic there, complained to me that as regards the small group teaching rooms, it was not quarts and pint pots but quarts and thimbles.

The growth was jet-propelled by the university (like all the others) needing student fees (particularly overseas fees) to thrive. Survive even. The student crowd enlarged and got lonelier. As the pioneer sociologist Émile Durkheim discovered, a major cause of suicide is *anomie*, a feeling of uprootedness of being in a 'society' but not in a community – *Gemeinschaft* in sociology-speak. 'Permanently withdrawn' in Sussex content-warning-speak.

There continued, despite these efforts, to be suicides at Sussex.[*] One, that of 22-year-old Daniel Bowen in late 2018, caught the press's attention. Daniel was a young, aspirant, man of colour studying chemistry – a field in which Sussex was a world leader.

Standards for students of the subject were high and unforgiving. Daniel was getting failing grades and penalties for handing in work late. He couldn't keep up. In desperation, he killed himself. His body, in the water at Brighton Marina, was not discovered for days.

The salient cause for his self-destruction was, reportedly, grades and what at his inquest were indicted as Sussex's 'draconian' standards and pastoral neglect of students who could not meet them. The university was criticised by the coroner at the inquest for its handling of Bowen's case. She noted that

---

[*] The suicide rate at Sussex was statistically less than for the age group nationally. But the student population is, generally, socially advantaged – a factor which works against suicide given future life prospects.

Bowen 'was registered with student support but that this only occurred after he wrote "tragically sad" poems in his Chemistry exams, days before his death'.

The court issued Sussex University with a Regulation 28 report. Such reports indicate that the coroner believes further action should be taken to prevent future deaths of the kind. They are reprimands. They hurt, not least in that they open institutions to legal action for failure of care.

In the student newspaper, it was noted that science subjects – where pass/fail is a more measurable threshold – induced greater stress than in humanities. Another student in 2018, Rajiv Aryal, enrolled in astrophysics, had killed himself.

A further Sussex suicide, in October 2020, again caught the metropolitan press's attention: namely that of Shubamso Pul, a first-year social science undergraduate. He, too, was living in a student residence (fondly believed to have a high 'buddy' quotient). He had evidently studied means of suicide online from the method he finally chose. He left a suicide note in which he exonerated anyone and the university from blame giving as reason: 'I don't like being alone, but I also want to be alone.'

It was against this background that, understandably, *Miss Julie* was withdrawn. But where should universities go? My own view, from having spent fifty years in that world, is simple: 'Small Is Beautiful'. The date (1973) of E. F. Schumacher's book dates me, of course, but the title and subtitle, *Small Is Beautiful: A Study of Economics as if People Mattered*, is surely as relevant to universities as the Treasury. 'Big is Efficient' is currently preferred. People? Let them take care of themselves.

'CANCELLED BY TWITTER'

Kosoko Jackson is a busy web advocate principally for the young adult (YA) product. Based in Washington DC, he identifies as multiply marginalised (in his own words: black, queer) and writes from within that zone in OwnVoices manner. He is edging creatively into full-time adult fiction. He knows the transitional fields intimately. He worked for major publishers in his early professional life as a sensitivity reader.

Jackson is in general sympathy with #OneVoice and links it to what one could call #OwnExperience. As he put it in a May 2018 tweet which went viral (Jackson lived to regret its stringency): 'Stories about the civil rights movement should be written by black people. Stories of suffrage should be written by women. Ergo, stories about boys during horrific and life changing times, like the AIDS EPIDEMIC, should be written by gay men. Why is this so hard to get?'

The clock and calendar are very hard on YA product.

Every teen year of growing 'up' is, in itself, 'an age'. YA ('young adult' – usually senior high school grade) has precise acronyms: MG: middle grade; NA: new adult: (just graduated high school). After that: aged out.

Nine months after laying down the law about authenticity and validatory experience, Kosoko Jackson embarked on his debut novel. It was styled 'YA' by him and his publisher, the fiercely independent Sourcebooks. Publication day was announced as 26 March 2019. Jackson would be by then closing in on thirty. Well beyond NA.

The novel was entitled *A Place for Wolves*. It generated good prepublication and proof-copy word of mouth and won a 'Kids' Indie Next' nomination. It would be read. It is the story of two queer boys of colour, one American, the other Brazilian. Jackson was within his ethical stockade with the love plot but not the historical setting – the late 1990s Kosovo conflict. The boys' quest is to make it to the safety of the American Embassy in Pristina as war rages around them.

The Kosovo Serbian–Albanian war was genocidally bloody. The lovers fall foul of a sadistic Albanian Muslim terrorist chief – the kind of brute who would feed a dying Serbian to his dogs. By name Beqiri, he is a one-man crime against humanity.

Jackson had broken his own golden rule. Born in 1991, he was a child when these atrocities were taking place. And a stranger to that place. He did not know the languages. His historical research was, at best, patchy and grossly wrong-headed. The civilian Albanian population suffered horrific massacres, rape, ethnic cleansing and a programme of cultural annihilation. It added up to genocide.*

Kosoko Jackson's apparent Albanophobia, Islamophobia and downright ignorance was excoriated on the Twitterverse. The publisher had released prepublication copies to Goodreads. Comment was led by a furious respondent of Albanian heritage who began: 'I have to be absolutely fucking honest here, everybody. I've never been so disgusted in my life.'

---

* There is a voluminous, historically grounded, I believe accurate Wikipedia entry.

Another capitalised their judgement: 'FUCKING YIKES, GET THIS SHIT AWAY FROM ME.' The denunciation circulated massively, becoming a Twitter hue and cry.

A Place for Wolves had been printed and published but was never distributed. Sourcebooks withdrew and pulped 55,000 copies. Jackson put out an accompanying statement to the 'book community':

> I failed to fully understand the people and the conflict that I set around my characters. I have done a disservice to the history and to the people who suffered … I apologize to those I hurt with my novel. I vow, moving forward, to do better and use this opportunity to grow.

The killing of the novel inspired disturbed articles in *Slate*, the *New Yorker* and the *New York Times*. What concerned commentators was not any offensiveness in the novel itself but its erasure: in the term which was becoming current, its cancellation.

Jackson waited until the anger subsided to publish his second novel, miscalled his 'debut', *Yesterday Is History*, in 2021. It is a fantasy about a liver transplant, the organ doubling as a time machine. Publishers stood by him, and he published three novels in 2022.

A Place for Wolves is available from Amazon at £107. It seems (as I write) that there is only one pre-owned copy in stock. Come buy.

FANNY HILL

On 12 August 2017, Judith Hawley, a professor at Royal Hollo-way London, was 'exposed' by the *Daily Mail* under the head-line: 'Erotic novel first banned 270 years ago for describing a young girl's sexual exploits is censored AGAIN – in case it upsets students. Professor Judith Hawley has revealed she has removed it from reading lists.'

The novel in question, *Fanny Hill* by John Cleland, had been long reprinted by Penguin Classics: it was filmed ('daringly') in 1983 and had been adapted, full frontal, for BBC Four in 2002. By 2017, for students hardened by access to hardcore pornography on their phones, its shock quotient was less than zero.

Hawley's reason for 'censoring' this bawdy 'classic' was given (mistakenly), by the *Mail*, as 'in case it upsets students'. The exposé was picked up by *The Times* and, bizarrely, *Vogue*. Tracked back, the *Mail*'s story originated in a passing remark Professor Hawley had made on a Radio 4 programme 'The Invention of Free Speech': 'In the 1980s I both protested against the opening of a sex shop in Cambridge and taught *Fanny Hill*. Nowadays I would be worried about causing offence to my students.'

The title, '*Fanny Hill*', is a recondite jest – the Englishing of the Latin '*mons veneris*', Mount of Venus, a circumlocution for the female pudendum. What the author, John Cleland, offered was in essence a jollied-up Hogarth's *Harlot's Progress* with a happy ending.

There are various versions of how it happened to be written.

One version is that John Cleland, a 'rake' to borrow another Hogarthism, found himself in debtors' prison in 1748 and wanted fast money (when published, *Fanny Hill* was a bestseller from the start). A more pleasing version is that it was the result of a jest with James Boswell (Dr Johnson's biographer) to prove that a libertine work could achieve its erotic effects without ever resorting to 'four-letter words' (also absent from Dr Johnson's great *Dictionary*).

In his *London Journal*, Boswell records a 1762 encounter with one of Fanny Hill's trade which has very much the same masculinist breeziness, bawdry and jolly euphemism as Cleland's novel:

> I had now been sometime in town without female sport ... I picked up a girl in the Strand and went into a court with intention to enjoy her in armour [with a sheepskin condom]. But she had none. I toyed with her. She wondered at my size, and said if I ever took a Girl's Maidenhead, I would make her squeak. I gave her a shilling; and had command enough of myself to go without touching her.

An unbrutal flagellation scene (*Fifty Shades of Grey* style) figured centrally in the prosecution of *Fanny Hill* on 8 November 1963 on charges of obscenity. Unlike *Lady Chat*, *Fanny Hill* was never acquitted – but in 1963, who cared?* The following is how Cleland describes the flagellation of Fanny:

---

* Constance Chatterley is called, by intimates, 'Connie' – like 'Fanny', a euphemism for female private parts. Lawrence evidently knew Cleland's novel.

All my back parts, naked half way up, were now fully at his mercy: and first, he stood at a convenient distance, delighting himself with a gloating survey of the attitude I lay in, and of all the secret stores I thus exposed to him in fair display. Then, springing eagerly towards me, he covered all those naked parts with a fond profusion of kisses; and now, taking hold of the rod, rather wantoned with me, in gentle inflictions on those tender trembling masses of my flesh behind.

How did Fanny get to this somewhat undignified position in life? As the narrative opens, she is a young fifteen-year-old just come up to London from the country. Smallpox has ravaged her family but not her face. In no sense is she 'deflowered'. She is adopted, as virgin chattel, on arrival, by an amiable procuress into her brothel and graduates to enjoy a profitable career and finally a good marriage. She brings with her no offspring or disease.*

Cleland's *Pretty Woman* contention is that 'women of pleasure' – 'whores' in franker eighteenth-century male terminology – have as much 'pleasure' in being trafficked as the men who use and discard them after use. It is George Bernard Shaw's contention in *Mrs Warren's Profession* and *Getting Married*. Matrimony? Prostitution? Same thing.

Shaw's too smart contention is, to borrow Orwell's word again, bollox. But bollox plus is the *Pretty Woman*, Richard

---

* I discuss her never-mentioned contraceptives and protectives in *Can Jane Eyre be Happy?* (1997).

Gere–Julia Roberts myth. In terms of literature's dealing with sex, there is much to ponder in *Fanny Hill*. Judith Hawley's prompt riposte to the *Mail* was thoughtful as she laid it out in a *Guardian* article of 15 August 2017. First off, she pointed out, the novel had never been on her course 'The Age of Oppositions, 1660–1780'. Dates had further significance. In the 1980s, an instructor could assume a degree of cultural homogeneity in her seminar. Greater cultural diversity in the now much larger and diverse student body entailed new kinds of mutual respect between lecturer and lectured to. 'Sensitivity teaching', to coin a phrase.

The other crucial factor was fees. When students were paying for the course almost as much as a junior lecturer was being paid for teaching it, a new authority balance was required – and with it new curricular variations. As Hawley put it (anticipating key arguments of #MeToo): 'The problem with teaching *Fanny Hill* is not to do with sex, but power. When senior academics make a work of pornography a set text, they should attend to the power relations implicit in the pedagogic relationship and be aware that students can feel coerced.'

Professor Hawley describes the eggshell path of the current university teacher neatly. But who, when it comes to triggering, has the 'power' in the current university? The payer or the paid? The teacher or the taught? The grader or the graded? If your students can't hack it but are still liable for eyewatering fees to be told it, can you fail them? If a section of the class finds male fantasies about what women feel when trafficked for sex beyond dignifying with discussion, do you, without any song and dance, choose a more appropriate text? Or just trigger and hope for the best.

SCOTT FREE

In the weekly causerie page of *The Spectator*, on 21 January 2023, Charles Moore, alerted by headlines in the *Daily Mail*, took issue with Warwick University. He had read, over the lazy days between Christmas 2022 and New Year, that the university's 'English department had issued trigger warnings to students against "offensive" passages in *Ivanhoe* about "people of colour" and the attribution to Muslims of anti-Semitic sentiments'.

Having turned his festive boredom to purpose, he told his readers: 'It is a benefit of wokery that it prompts one to look anew. I was always slightly ashamed that I had never read a novel by Walter Scott.' As the wearily reiterated jest puts it, the once 'Great Unknown' of the nineteenth century is in the twenty-first century the 'Great Unread'.

Moore dusted off his works of Scott, lying years virgin on his shelves, and got to work on *Ivanhoe*, his lance upraised and targeting the Warwick softies. The joust was on:

The much more important point is that the most gripping part of [*Ivanhoe*'s] narrative is its vivid assault on anti-Semitism, personified in the superb character of Rebecca, daughter of the usurer, Isaac of York – sexy, brave, strong yet modest, loving a Gentile (I won't tell you who), but faithful to her Judaism. I have rarely read a more truly anti-racist novel. Of this, the Warwick woke wardens make no mention.

(The spoiler alert is a nice touch.)

I hail Moore for stirring *Ivanhoe*'s embers to find a live spark or two in the twelfth-century medieval fantasia. But one might add a further cause for triggering which escaped his notice. Namely, that the author of *Ivanhoe*, largely through *Ivanhoe*, can be held responsible for the death of 750,000 Americans and their then President, Honest Abe Lincoln. To the racism Warwick piously indicts, one can add the propagation of lethal myth.

Scott's fiction soaked into the nineteenth-century American worldview like rain into sponge. 'Scott mania', literary historians call it. No one until the end of his career in the late 1820s knew for certain that Walter Scott was the author of the hitherto bestselling fiction ever written. That invisible person was given on title pages as 'The Author of *Waverley*'. He was a fascinating unknown as much as the Black Knight who dominates the action of *Ivanhoe* (King Richard the Lionheart, as it happens).

There are twelve towns in America called Ivanhoe and twenty-seven called Waverley. Street names after Scott novels and characters abound in every major city. *Ivanhoe* was so popular, and horses so available, that medieval tournaments were organised in southern towns in the 1830s, closely following *Ivanhoe*'s script.

Mark Twain called America's nineteenth-century love affair with Scott the 'Sir Walter disease'. His lethal infection was, Twain averred, administered in two stages. First off, Scott, as Twain alleges, confected the antebellum 'grand illusions' which led to the Civil War. *Ivanhoe*, particularly, was responsible. As Twain writes in *Life on the Mississippi*:

> Then comes Sir Walter Scott with his enchantments ... sets the world in love with dreams and phantoms; with decayed and swinish forms of religion; with decayed and degraded systems of government; with the sillinesses and emptinesses, sham grandeurs, sham gauds, and sham chivalries of a brainless and worthless long-vanished society.
>
> He did measureless harm; more real and lasting harm, perhaps, than any other individual that ever wrote ... It was Sir Walter that made every gentleman in the South a Major or a Colonel, or a General or a Judge, before the war; and it was he, also, that made these gentlemen value these bogus decorations.

Scott, among all the rest, is responsible for the phony Elvis's 'Colonel' Tom Parker and the finger lickin' 'good ole boy' Kentucky Fried Chicken's 'Colonel' Sanders.

Twain goes further in his *j'accuse*:

> Sir Walter had so large a hand in making Southern character, as it existed before the war, that he is in great measure responsible for the war. It seems a little harsh toward a dead

man to say that we never should have had any war but for Sir Walter; and yet something of a plausible argument might, perhaps, be made in support of that wild proposition.

The author of *Huckleberry Finn* hated the author of *Waverley*. Not for what he wrote but for what he unintentionally did.[*]

Secondly, as Twain saw it, Sir Walter's influence continued in the American south even more poisonously after the Civil War. He was the invisible hand behind the Invisible Empire, the Ku Klux Klan – those postbellum nostalgists who yearned (fragments still yearn) for the white, Christian 'Saxon' antebellum supremacy, flavoured with tartan: a sartorial absurdity invented by Scott out of the simple Scottish 'plaid'.

The fiery cross – signalling the rising of the clans to battle in Scott's poem 'The Lady of the Lake' – was adopted by the Klan: as image and act. Klansmen saw themselves as knights errant. American Celts were known as the 'blue blood of the south'. The Scottish Scott was one of their father figures. African Americans were at the bottom of the American racial hierarchy. It translated into white masters and black slaves as something as natural as American exceptionalism and manifest destiny. Or haggis for supper.

Following the defeat of the southern states in the Civil War, it was a caucus of six former Confederate officers of Scottish and Irish descent (Celts) who formed the KKK militia in 1865. The brothers Frank and Luther McCord helped form the first

---

[*] Twain's highly unromantic, more historically correct, version of English early medievalism is given in *A Connecticut Yankee in King Arthur's Court* (1889).

Klan chapter but embossed it, in honour of their name, with the Scottish thistle.

The chivalric glamour of the KKK in the first half of the twentieth century was given a huge boost by the filmically epic, ideologically obnoxious film *The Birth of a Nation* (1915). It was originally entitled by its maker, D. W. Griffith, *The Clansman*. It is the saga of the post-war south which will and must rise again as it formerly was. The climactic scenes show the Klan, in full fig, riding in to save the old south (and its pure maidenhood) from the black savages whom defeat and the north has put in power.

One can dispute Twain's hyperbolic claims about Scott and his inspiring the Civil War. But the author of *Huckleberry Finn* knew the south and sensed the importance of the Scottophile Klan. It became immensely strong politically in the 1920s, representing a real threat to democracy. It was brought down, like Al Capone, by tax delinquency. It remains in the shadows to this day, like the ashes of the phoenix, ready to be reborn when the fiery cross brings it back to life.

This notion of southern knighthood, and romantic Caledonianism, survives in the modern US, with all its 'Scotland' paraphernalia (less *Ivanhoe* than *Rob Roy* nowadays). In a witty article in *Atlanta Magazine* on 14 October 2021, Jim Galloway recalls being brought up in the deep south in a milieu as distantly Scoto-American as his own two names. That milieu has lived on, he says:

Georgia is on the cusp of a new season of caber-tossing.

For nearly five decades, usually on the third weekend of the month, October has hosted the 'Stone Mountain Highland Games' ... Scores of men whose legs are well past their prime – and not a few women – will don kilts and tipple whisky ... With bagpipes, dance, athletics, and the serious perusal of souvenir stands, all will celebrate what they know of Scottish history and culture. And all will happen on the site of what is likely the most egregious corruption of Scottish history and culture ever to occur on this continent.

It was on 25 November 1915 (concurrent with D. W. Griffith's movie) that a flaming cross 'atop Stone Mountain announced the rebirth of the Ku Klux Klan'. That event is still commemorated annually.

A tiny strand of the 'Sir Walter disease' in Trumpism is signalled in his echt Scottish forename, 'Donald'. As the web tells us: 'Donald is a masculine given name derived from the Gaelic name Dòmhnall. This comes from the Proto-Celtic Dumno-ualos ("world-ruler" or "world-wielder").'

He wishes.

AN AMERICAN MARRIAGE: TAYARI JONES

Endorsement ('read this!') is the reverse side of triggering and content warning ('be wary when reading this'). Tayari Jones's novel, published in 2018, was endorsed – as proclaimed on the dust jacket of softcover editions – by the once most powerful man in the world. It was, said President Obama: 'A moving portrayal of the effects of a wrongful conviction on a young African-American couple'. Rhetoric, of MLK power, was never Barack's gift.

The young African American couple have been married for eighteen months. They are middle-class, college-educated professionals. On a visit to the husband's parents in deep south Louisiana, they overnight in a seedy motel. Late at night, he helps a middle-aged woman with an injured arm at the landing's ice machine. Is she white? Or is she black? The novel does not tell us.

Not all America has arrived at the twenty-first century. The police arrive mob-handed. The husband is railroaded on a rape charge. The woman on the landing's allegation is the sole evidence, and he is given twelve years' hard time. The accuser does not figure as a character – we know nothing about her other than that she is 'heavyset, with a kind, dimpled face'. It's not an omission; it's a test imposed by the author on the reader.

The nature of the test is the root CRT (critical race theory) contention: that racism is not something superficial. It is in-grained and you yourself may not know it's there, until you're tested. Like the faulty gene in your DNA which gives you cancer.*

What, the reader of *An American Marriage* is asked, do you see on the landing? It defines you. White or black – or something other? Most readers will, I think, see white. There could, of course, be a plot twist – it's a black woman. But then (we're

---

* I confess that on first reading I assumed that the woman on the landing must have been white.

deep into CRT here) would a black man get twelve years in the deep south for raping a black woman? We'll never know. But, the author intends, we shall – having finished the novel – know ourselves better.

There's more than one kind of prejudice of the CRT kind. Take, for example, the following riddle, presented by Rich Barlow's Boston University website: a father and son are in a car and crash; the father is killed. The son is rushed to hospital and prepared for surgery. When the boy's mask is removed, the surgeon shouts: 'My God, I can't operate – he's my son!'

Stop here. What was your automatic visualisation of the operating theatre? The surgeon, of course, is his mother. Two Boston University psychologists ran an experiment on the riddle on some 200 of their students and discovered only 15 per cent solved the riddle.

It's taken as a classic instance of gender bias – whose explanation is the same as CRT. It lurks.

A final illustrative riddle about ingrained bias. It's historical and I take it from Sam Miller's book *Migrants* (2023). Joseph Kearney was an Irish shoemaker, in the little village of Moneygall. In the great famine of the 1840s, like millions of other Irishmen, he emigrated to America and settled, with his family, in Ohio. The Kearneys thrived. One of his direct descendants became President of the United States. Who was he: Reagan? Clinton? Kennedy? Biden?

None of them. It is Barack Obama, 'the great-great-great-great-grandson of Joseph Kearney, the shoemaker of

Moneygall'. You, like many, perhaps forgot that Obama's mother, Dr Ann Dunham, was white.

T. S. ELIOT TRIGGERED

In November 2022, T. S. Eliot, enacted on stage, was subjected to a triggering which qualifies as theatre of the absurd. It was perpetrated in and by a theatre – the Arcola in Dalston, London.

Chris Hastings, by now the country's Trigger-Finder General (and very adept at it), exposed this latest nonsense in the *Mail on Sunday* under the headline: 'March of the Woke Warriors: The Craziest Trigger Warning Yet!'

Read on and splutter was the implied instruction.

The play in question, *Dinner with Groucho*, imagines a meeting between Groucho Marx and T. S. Eliot, over a dinner table, in an afterlife restaurant. Both eminent diners were well dead. It is a kind of Sartrean *huis clos* played for laughs. The author was Irish playwright Frank McGuinness, a dab hand at bio-fantasia. The play ran for a few months in the UK and went on to attract sell-out performances in Dublin and Belfast.

Triggers, of a bizarre kind, abounded. Those who bought their tickets by post received them with the warning that the play 'Contains Use of Haze and Prop Cigars'. Was 'prop' a misprint for 'proper'? No: on entering the auditorium, the audience were confronted by a large sign with the same warning. And, if they still didn't get it, the warning was reprinted in the programme.

It was all anticlimactic. If the audience expected the tip of Groucho's old cigar to glow, it did so battery powered. There was no naked flame but a lot of pyrophobia that winter in the Arcola Theatre. Strange. Had they all been smoking something else behind stage?

A spokesperson told the *Mail on Sunday* (was she pulling Hastings's plonker?): 'The Government's Health and Safety Executive recommends that entertainment venues using smoke or haze in productions should print warnings on or with the tickets and post warning notices on the premises. This is standard practice across London.'

But was there a health and safety regulation on fake, battery-operated cigars? Was the fear that the audience would stampede to the exits mistaking them for the real thing?

There was predictable frothing from luvvies. *Downton Abbey* creator Julian Fellowes sighed: 'I simply do not understand the fashion for infantilising an audience, treating them as if they were three years old.' Maureen Lipman tartly quipped: 'Groucho Marx without a cigar is like a footballer without a tattoo – and it should be a lit cigar.' Were they, though, being taken for a ride?

Tom and Groucho met only once in life, but they corresponded, much to each other's amusement (Nobel Prize meets Vaudeville). Their relationship began when Eliot wrote a fan letter requesting a signed photograph in 1961. He wanted to put it up on his office wall at Faber's publishing house, he said, alongside his fellow Nobellist, the utterly humourless W. B. Yeats. A private joke.

The one meeting, a dinner party for one guest (Groucho), took place at Eliot's London flat in June 1964; his second wife, Valerie, fussed over the occasion. She was soon, after his death, to be the keeper of the Eliot flame. She made sure, for the whole of her long life, that no publishing rascal got within sight of Tom's personal history. He left no known record of dinner with Groucho. Groucho did: grouchily.

Eliot admired the Marx Brothers as much as he loved English music hall – many of its grandest buildings now, in the 1960s, converted to cinemas, clubs and bingo halls. The Marx Brothers had dominated post-talkie comedy film as joyously as Marie Lloyd (who is mentioned in McGuinness's play) or cheeky-chappie Max Miller did the British music hall boards. It was a proletarian *élan vital* the enervated patrician Eliot envied. His own life force ran thin. By the 1960s, poetry had run out of him as well.

The incendiary cigar was a key part of Groucho's Jewish schmutter along with the forename ('kvetcher', groucher), the Einstein moustache and the frock coat. The Marx Brothers were first-generation New Yorkers – only Groucho played Jewish, to the hilt, and, unlike Al Jolson, unsentimentally.

The Marx Brothers (their father changed the family name) were brought up, as kids, on Manhattan's Upper East Side New York – an Italian district. There is revenge for the Jew-baiting they got in their vowel-ended names – Chico, Gummo, Harpo, Zeppo – all are dumb as two planks: except for Groucho who wisecracks in every line smart. And, with the glowing phallic symbol in his mouth, is lecherous, a Jewish Casanova.

Unlike later globally famous film and radio comedians (Bob Hope, for example – who borrowed a lot from Groucho), he did not have scriptwriters. In the free-wheeling twenty-first century he might, if Bob Dylan qualified, have been nominated for a Nobel and joined T. S. Eliot in the Swedish pantheon.

As a person, Groucho was secretly mortified, his biographer tells us, at his lack of higher education and 'class'. He ingrained that mortification into his aggressive comic persona. Eliot, who had no shortage of education, chain smoked (elegantly). Tidy mountains of white ash would rise in the tray next to where he sat. Visiting the poet Stephen Spender, Eliot admired the transparently crystal cigarette case his host had. Spender sent it to him the next day, with an elegant *vers d'occasion*.

Eliot responded with his own verse the day after, thanking his disciple for 'the fair transparency'. It thereafter resided on his coffee table. Smoking was a big thing in Eliot's life. And his death. He died, prematurely, of emphysema.

Looking back on the Arcola event, I suspect the folderol about cigars and haze was a decoy, a red herring. There was an elephant in the auditorium. There should have been another trigger – but it was too hot to handle. By 2022–23, Eliot had been exposed, indicted, charged and – despite a desperate rear-guard action – convicted in the public mind of antisemitism. The evidence was well known – most of it on the page. But the closing speech for the prosecution was the distinguished lawyer Anthony Julius's *T. S. Eliot, Anti-Semitism and Literary Form* (1995).

Julius goes to the core of what himself Eliot believed

doctrinally, what was central to his poetic self. One example will serve. In 1934, Eliot published a collection of his miscellaneous prose under the book title *After Strange Gods*. It has an Old Testament prophetic ring to it.* In it, Eliot declares, as his view manifestly:

> The population should be homogeneous; where two or more cultures exist in the same place they are likely either to be fiercely self-conscious or both to become adulterate. What is still more important is unity of religious background, and reasons of race and religion combine to make any large number of free-thinking Jews undesirable.

Hitler had come to power in the same months that *After Strange Gods* was published. It is not hard to find parallel passages in *Mein Kampf*. It doesn't come up in the play, other than, as reviewers noted, a tension between the main characters – letters worked; face to face didn't.

Theatres work by creating and manipulating effect. The Arcola management were sophisticated theatre people. What the nonsense about fake cigars was insinuating was that there was something dangerous or sinister – but work it out. What was it Freud said (supposedly), 'Sometimes a cigar is just a cigar'? Sometimes, if it comes as a trigger warning, it isn't. It's the invisible elephant.

---

* Aaron, Exodus 32:4 on the Israelites' false idols: 'These *be* thy gods, O Israel, which brought thee up out of the land of Egypt.'

IOWA'S *INDEX OF LIBRORUM PROHIBITORUM*

In September 2022, for the start of the new academic year, the University of Iowa's general education literature programme chose *Kindred*, by Octavia E. Butler, to be their 'feature title 'for a second year' running. It meant that all students would have it prescribed or recommended.

The hope was that the novel would enlighten the coming generation on questions of race and create a lifelong (or, at least, degree-long) reading habit. The prescription was 'geared' towards English non-majors. Not, nowadays, a widely great-novel reading class.

Kindred, meanwhile, continued to be a 'blacklisted' (in two senses) book in Iowa's state and federal prisons. Books by any black author (including Barack Obama's *Dreams from My Father* and Michelle Obama's *Becoming*) are routinely blocked in prisons, lest they stir up resentments about why there are so many black faces in the prison and its library. In Iowa, African Americans constituted 4 per cent of state residents but 20 per cent of people in jail and 24 per cent of people in prison. Since 1970, the total jail population has increased 522 per cent to the same proportions.

Octavia E. Butler is one of a pioneering cohort of late twentieth-century African American writers who fought to get the literary black voice heard. They succeeded, being one of the signal victories of twentieth-century literature, as much an achievement as USSR samizdat literature. Unlike Maya

Angelou, Toni Morrison, James Baldwin and Alex Haley (all of whose books, like Butler's, were unable to squeeze through prison bars), her genre was science fiction/fantasy.

Kindred is Dana's story. She is an African American southern Californian tyro writer who is married to a white professional. They are a rising middle-class couple: the world at their feet. Race? No big deal in Los Angeles or San Francisco. The date of the action is summer 1976: the bicentennial year. The thesis of the novel is that, in celebrating 'Independence', white America had wilfully fanfared out its outrageous black American history. *Kindred* coincided with Alex Haley's *Roots*, and the immensely watched TV follow-up in 1977.

The hero of Butler's novel, Dana, has 'dizzy spells' in which she and later her husband Kevin are time-transported back to early nineteenth-century Maryland, and a slave-worked plantation. There is a complex, 'butterfly effect' central plot.*

Dana saves, on each of her time travels, the life of Rufus, the white heir apparent to the property in which she is chattel. It emerges Rufus is her ancestor; lest she negate herself, she has to arrange the virtual rape of a female, black ancestor. The morality of the novel is intricate and defies easy interpretation. Its power lies in the shocking (and, one is convinced, wholly authentic) depictions of what slavery felt like to slaves. And how evil it was.

---

* Ray Bradbury's 1952 short story ('The Sound of Thunder') in which, on a time travel trip, a tourist accidentally treads on a butterfly. He returns to the present only to find it horribly changed. The story's basic idea was filmed as *The Butterfly Effect* (2005).

The list of 'triggers' on the website Book Trigger Warnings are as follows: 'Abuse (physical and sexual); Ableism (r-slur); Amputation; Attempted rape; Family separation (forced); Loss of a child; Lynching; Racial slurs (N-word); Racism; Rape (mentioned); Slavery; Suicide; Violence (graphic); Whipping'. The history of white American on African American abuse is encapsulated in those terms.

It's a great novel which – as skilfully as does Margaret Atwood in *The Handmaid's Tale* – uses a genre which seldom aims high. Atwood's theme is gender, not racial, slavery. Butler's novel will, academics feel, do good in Iowa higher education, and prison governors think differently about what it might do in their domains where, unlike America as a whole, African Americans have ceased being a minority. At the period Butler first published *Kindred* (the '70s), more young black people were in prison than at college.

THE ROMEO AND JULIET EFFECT

Romeo and Juliet was first performed in 1597, scholars think. It belongs to Shakespeare's early phase, before the original Globe was opened. It is, in the largest sense, a play about the war between young and old. Age wins.

Flash forward to 2021 and Shakespeare's restored Globe Theatre on the Thames South Bank. The Royal Shakespeare Company mounted a new adaptation of *Romeo and Juliet* in modern dress, setting and a multi-ethnic cast. The performance was accompanied with a 'trigger' handout to the incoming audience, warning that 'this production contains depictions of suicide, moments of violence and references to drug use. It contains gunshot sound effects and the use of stage blood.'

For those who were disturbed by what they saw onstage, the Samaritans' helpline number and details of the Listening Place – a mental health charity – were given.

'Trauma survivors' were specifically mentioned by the theatre management when asked why they had done it. It was not feared that the audience en masse would go lemming. The fear was that the play would 'trigger' PTSD in survivors of self-harm or victims of abusive harm by others.

'Barmy', 'mollycoddling' and 'snowflakery' were the *Daily Mail*'s 'common sense' barrage among a chorus of scornful response to the RSC's content warning. But was this triggering of *Romeo and Juliet* barmy? There is a lot of suicide in Shakespeare's plays – 'to be or not to be?' is a question which hangs over much of the corpus. But the self-destruction in *Romeo and Juliet* is unique in its being a *suicide à deux* inspired by love not Hamletian *Weltschmerz*. As staged, it is a positive, even an exalting act. And contagiously beautiful.

In the play's climax, one young lover thinks the body of his beloved is now a corpse. Romeo's lament may be seen as romantic or faintly necrophiliac:

> O my love, my wife,
> Death, that hath sucked the honey of thy breath,
> Hath had no power yet upon thy beauty:
> Thou art not conquered, beauty's ensign yet

> Is crimson in thy lips and in thy cheeks
> And Death's pale flag is not advancèd there.

Romeo poisons himself alongside the body, having just killed his rival lover of Juliet, Paris, who has also arrived at the unofficial mausoleum arranged by bumbling Friar Laurence.

Juliet duly wakes up from her non-lethal (as it emerges) poison and – facing life without Romeo (his corpse and that of Paris lying in front of her) – takes up Romeo's (not Paris's) dagger and stabs herself through the heart: the organ of love. She falls dead – not for her any prolonged Cleopatra-like suicide farewell. She is in a hurry to join Romeo. In a production I have seen, she falls on his body. It is their second act of carnal love.

The dagger's sexual implication is manifest. Lest we miss it, Juliet says she will 'sheath' the weapon in herself. The Latin 'vagina' translates as 'sheath or scabbard'. She is, the play has earlier told us, thirteen years old. Romeo sixteen. The RSC does not impose any age-restriction on its performances other than adult company with the very young. There would have been teens in the audience. They could be seen as particularly vulnerable to the young lovers' suicide pact.

Alphira and Christopher Stonehouse married in 2005. They were not teenagers. He was older than she. Both had histories of mental health issues, although their marriage was, apparently, happy. The couple possessed a DVD of Franco Zeffirelli's 1968 film of *Romeo and Juliet*. On a bitterly cold night in November 2012, Alphira and Christopher played the tape. Afterwards, they went to their bedroom and poisoned themselves; as do Romeo and Juliet. A text of the play was found alongside their bodies, with passages highlighted. It was Alphira's suicide note.

A message was pinned on their flat's door with the instruction: 'Unless you are the Emergency Services, Do Not Enter. Alphira and Chris, aka Romeo and Juliet'. Christopher Stonehouse's joint suicide note, alongside their bodies, stated: 'Alphira and I have chosen to end our lives. We have suffered for too long and cannot bear it any longer. Our backdoor and gate are unlocked.'

The point here is not that Shakespeare's play inspired Alphira and Chris but that it gave shape and form to how they composed their final desperate act. Perhaps it even brought a small degree of comfort. It made their self-erasure significant – something that 'mattered'. They (actually calling themselves Romeo and Juliet, not Mr and Mrs Stonehouse) were playing a part.

Zeffirelli's film became headline news again in 2022–23. The two British actors who had played the leads, Olivia Hussey and Leonard Whiting, were then fifteen (she) and sixteen (he). There was no chaperonage on set. The post-marital bedroom scene – in which his buttocks and her breasts are lingered on by Zeffirelli's camera – were much remarked on and regarded as the film's 'money shot'. The sales pitch was that the actors were, true to Shakespeare's text, barely more than children. The scene can be found on the web, but you must hunt for it after the scene was alleged, fifty years later, to be child abusive.

It being the morally relaxed late '60s, the film was not censored on its first release. It came out in 1968 with a 'G' rating, which meant no age restriction whatsoever. It was rerated PG (parental guidance) in 1973, when things were tightening up morally. Edited school prints (less buttocks, breasts and cleavage) were available for those of Hussey's and Whiting's age.

In 2022–23, Hussey and Whiting, now in their early seventies sued for child abuse. If the case went the actors' way, possession of the scene, lodged on your hard drive, or possession of the unedited DVD which the Stonehouses had, could be construed as criminal. *Autres temps, autres mœurs.*

Most of the other actors who played alongside Hussey and Whiting were dead. Normally a statute of limitation would have prevented them from bringing the lawsuit for a now half-century-old offence. But California – in response to adults claiming childhood abuse from Catholic priests – had temporarily suspended their statute. It was due to come back in on 31 December 2022. Hussey and Whiting got their papers delivered to California's Justice Departments hours before closure on the 30th of the month.

Zeffirelli had died, much lauded, in 2019. The complaint was, necessarily, directed against the studio, Paramount, charging 'sexual abuse, sexual harassment and fraud'. This was not the anything-goes '60s. The studio had done well financially and reputationally with their *Romeo and Juliet*. The film had won or been nominated for four academy awards and the two young actors had been awarded Golden Globes.

The gist of the actors' case was simple. They charged that

Paramount Pictures had sexually exploited them and distributed nude images of children (i.e. them) or, at least, of fifteen-
year-old Hussey. Franco Zeffirelli was centrally implicated.
The actors claimed that before contract (parental consent
was required), the director (known on set as 'maestro' and
notoriously lecherous) had assured the youngsters and their
custodians there would be no nudity in the scene in which, as
Shakespeare portrays it, Juliet, as day breaks, implores Romeo
to make love to her again.

The couple, Zeffirelli had said, would do the scene wearing
flesh-coloured undergarments with discreet camera work.
Nevertheless, in the final crunch days of shooting, over budget,
the director pressured Hussey and Whiting to perform stark
naked, with only skimpy bed covering of genitals. The scene
is erotically lingered on in the movie. If they did not assent,
Zeffirelli said, 'the picture would fail' – and with it the kids'
future careers. It was non-consensual, non-contractual and
manifestly coercive.

'What they were told and what went on were two different
things,' said the actors' current (2023) business manager. 'They
trusted Franco. At 16, as actors, they took his lead that he
would not violate that trust they had. Franco was their friend,
and frankly, at 16, what [could] they do?'

According to their complaint, Hussey and Whiting had
suffered mental anguish in the half-century since the film's
release, during careers which after the triumph of *Romeo and
Juliet* were not stellar. Because of that one scene, it was alleged.
They sought damages said to be in excess of $500 million.

193

In May 2023, a Los Angeles judge dismissed the lawsuit. Hussey and Whiting said they would continue to fight for justice. Their case touches on a perennially sore point in *Romeo and Juliet*. In the original play, Juliet is, as the text makes clear, thirteen years old. Romeo, putatively, is sixteen.

At Shakespeare's Globe in the early seventeenth century, young boys with unbroken voices would play female parts. They would be quite likely younger than thirteen. Authenticity is nowadays a sacred rule on the London stage. The productions I saw in the '60s of Laurence Olivier doing Othello (apparently he blacked his covered chest as well as his face) and Shylock would be hard to stage in the 2020s.

It is a sign of the times that in summer 2022 Arthur Hughes became the first disabled actor at the Royal Shakespeare Company to play Richard III. The thirty-year-old actor was born with radial dysplasia, meaning he has a shorter right arm. The performance was applauded. But a pubescent thirteen-year-old actress playing Juliet is unthinkable.

Authenticity, however, has its contemporary elasticities. In a Globe production in September 2021, Rebekah Murrell, who played Juliet, was born in 1992. She is a woman of African heritage and London upbringing. She was sixteen years past the authenticity threshold, and that no one in sixteenth-century Verona would comment on her complexion is unlikely: Romeo describes Juliet as a gleaming star, putting the darkness of night to shame.

Murrell had read English literature at Manchester

University. She interpreted the part and keyed herself into a play whose modern Globe performance was, as she put, 'Brechtian ... not a usual Shakespeare production'. Her personal performance was praised by critics. Any inauthenticity aroused no comment.

What was innovative – Brechtian – about the Globe's production was that it incorporated its trigger warnings into the text itself. In Brecht's Theater am Schiffbauerdamm in postwar East Berlin, banners behind the actors would make the point of the scene. The *London Evening Standard* reviewer, Nick Curtis, was not won over at director Ola Ince (a very new broom at the RSC) having inserted 'jarring directorial intrusions' into the drama:

> At regular intervals, characters step forward to intone statements – that 20 per cent of young people experience depression before adulthood, that patriarchy is bad, that emotional neglect is a killer – which then sit emblazoned on a video screen until the next one comes along. Sometimes these relate to the play, sometimes to social mores, sometimes to [UK] government policy. All of them stop the otherwise propulsive action stone dead, every time.

That Verona's machete-packing teenagers are shown high on cocaine much of the time did not warrant video emblazoning. *Autres temps, autres Shakespeare.*

BRIDESHEAD: VISIT, PAY UP, REPENT!

Country house literature is a rich strand in English works: from Marvell's Appleton House, Austen's Mansfield Park and Dickens's Bleak House to Forster's Howards End, James's Poynton, Waugh's Brideshead (supposedly Castle Howard), Peake's Gormenghast (for those with a taste for Gothic) and Fellowes's Downton Abbey (for cultural nostalgists).

The English novel loves to dream of Manderley. Typically, the 'pile' (of bricks, not money) releases meditation on the aristocracy, dynasty, power elites, potentates and captains of industry. The master class.

The Englishman's home is his castle, says the proverb, but some Englishmen's homes really are castles. Many of them have proved too expensive for descendants to keep up and have fallen into the care of the National Trust. They were theirs; now they are ours.

The National Trust was founded in 1895 to acquire and preserve buildings and land of 'historic interest' and/or 'natural beauty'. The founders, male and female, were cultural leaders and philanthropists imbued with a refined patriotism and unbridled pride in Britain's world conquest: specifically, its still mighty empire – the largest the world had known. The National Trust's holdings, growing by the year, have become the most dispersed museum in Britain.

Monuments endure. Times change. In September 2020, a new blood management at the National Trust commissioned and published a 115-page 'interim report' on the places and collections it holds 'on behalf of the nation' identifying 'direct and indirect links to colonialism and historic slavery'. It did not include its natal 1895 self in the survey, but the subtext was shame at the NT for celebrating what should be sackcloth, ashes and scraping boils with shards.

Ninety-three properties were found to be tainted.

They were duly triggered – the wrecking ball not being appropriate. Future fee-paying visitors (a vital source of National Trust income) would be reminded by docents and signs of the black, now indispersible cloud over this particular national treasure. Indeed, every one of them – from circular Ickworth to, doubtless, the reed beds of Walberswick, home of the booming bittern. It was the leper cry and clapper: 'Unclean! Unclean!'

As the main author of the report, Dr Corinne Fowler (now professor of colonialism and heritage at Leicester University) proclaimed: visitors to National Trust sites would henceforth 'be increasingly confronted with uncomfortable truths at Britain's historic properties … Staff and volunteers will be urged to educate the public about the imperial exploitation which has propped up many heritage sites.'

'Uncomfortable truths' would put the ouch into the family outing.

The report provoked uproar. There ensued riotous NT AGMs, thunderous denunciation by the right-wing press and a flood of cancelled subscriptions (or threats to do so). If the new brooms at the National Trust wanted to brush up a storm, they succeeded. The then Culture Secretary, Oliver Dowden,

declared from aloft that the custodians of the country's heritage bodies had a duty to defend their legacy from those who
would 'do Britain down'. As for doing down, Hilary McGrady,
the National Trust's director general, received death threats, as
did Dr Fowler.

Those more coolly regarding the furore with literary sentiments might feel the National Trust's research team had
cast their net too wide. Rudyard Kipling's country house,
Bateman's, a fine building of Jacobean origin in the East Sussex
Weald, was branded as stained by colonialism and the slave
trade. Not because the building or its builders had, as far as
could be found, any material benefit from those two iniquities
but because Rudyard Kipling had owned and been resident
there with his wife from 1902 to 1939. That was thirty-seven
years of the building's nearly 400 years' existence. Mr and Mrs
Kipling passed through it, one might say, staying a little longer
than most National Trust visitors.

Kipling had received no personal benefit from colonialism
nor slavery. Indeed, as his poem 'Galley Slaves' proclaims, he
loathed the practice and maintained the British Empire had
been instrumental in abolishing it. His belief can be questioned but that is what Rudyard Kipling believed.

Examples of pro-colonialism can be plucked almost everywhere in the Kipling *oeuvre*. But what is taken as clinching
evidence of his racism is his poem, whose title has become his
albatross, 'The White Man's Burden'. He published it in 1899.
In it he foresees, with the turn of the century, the decline and

fall of the British Empire. The Anglo-Saxon mission, he demands, must be taken up by America, about to go to imperial war in the Philippines (a horribly cruel conflict, powerfully forgotten by Americans, but not Filipinos, in modern times). He prophesies, correctly as history proved, that the twentieth would be America's century.

The poem disgusts most modern readers of every complexion, with verses such as the following, addressed to America's then belligerently WASP leaders:

> Take up the White Man's burden –
> Send forth the best ye breed –
> Go, bind your sons to exile
> To serve your captives' need;
> On fluttered folk and wild –
> Your new-caught sullen peoples,
> Half devil and half child.

The National Trust's explanation for adding Bateman's to their list of shame was because 'the British Empire was a central theme and context of his literary output'. There are, the Kipling Society would aver, many other themes.

Nonetheless, Kipling is a prickly author for the twenty-first century and hard to like. In his own time, he was very liked. He was the first Englishman to win the Nobel Prize for Literature (uncontroversially) and is still the youngest laureate, at forty-one, ever.

Kipling's remained a powerful voice, when patriotism was vitally important, during the Second World War. A war, at its outset, between the British Empire and the German Reich. T. S. Eliot, who had elected to stay in the UK during the hostilities – aware that he might be on the Gestapo death list after invasion – brought out a volume of Kipling's poetry in December 1941: at the height of the Blitz. It was conceived an antidote to gloom and despondency.

In a long prefatory essay, Eliot does not mention the British Empire once. He presents and praises Kipling as a modern troubadour. In his 'Barrack-Room Ballads', Kipling spoke for, to and with the 'other ranks' of England. His verse had the folkish fibre of the English proletarian music hall (Eliot loved music hall singers like Marie Lloyd; hers was the earthy poetry of the people which Kipling, in his ballads, could only mimic – but which he mimicked pitch perfect).

Reviewing Eliot's volume, Orwell – who had also elected to risk his life by staying in England – sourly described Kipling as a 'good bad poet'. The bad has, in contemporary times, floated to the surface, and the good sunk like a stone leaving barely a ripple behind.

Kipling dethroned from his pedestal (his admired Rhodes still stood outside Oriel College) made headlines in 2018. Manchester University had refurbished its student union for its now 40,000-odd strong student body. It was decided, by a staff committee (without student representation or consultation, reportedly), to decorate the union's foyer with a mural panel on which was printed Kipling's much-quoted moral anthem, 'If'. It was written in 1895 and opens:

> If you can keep your head when all about you
> Are losing theirs and blaming it on you

It continues with a series of conditional verses each opening with 'If you ... etc.' So far, so good. But the last couple of lines are highly objectionable:

> Yours is the Earth and everything that's in it,
> And – which is more – you'll be a Man, my son!

The word 'man', in this kind of context, is a red flag in the twenty-first century, and taking over the earth is a nod towards Britain having, in Kipling's lifetime, taken over a quarter of the globe and, when the poem was written, still being hungry for a bigger slice under the aegis of Queen and Empress Victoria. Manchester's current student body is multi-ethnic and its sexes and genders are diverse.

Infuriated students whitewashed the Kipling poem into oblivion (whitewash was a nice touch) and inscribed, in its place, Maya Angelou's black pride anthem to African American insurgency, 'Still I Rise' (1978).

The explanation given by Manchester's righteous daubers was that Kipling 'dehumanised people of colour'. As reported by *The Guardian*, Sara Khan, the student union's liberation and access officer, noted that students had not been consulted about the art that would decorate the union building:

> We, as an exec[utive] team, believe that Kipling stands for the opposite of liberation, empowerment and human rights – the things that we, as an S[tudent] U[nion], stand for. [Kipling is] well known as author of the racist poem 'The White Man's Burden', and a plethora of other work that sought to legitimate the British empire's presence in India and dehumanise people of colour, it is deeply inappropriate to promote the work of Kipling in our SU, which is named after prominent South African anti-apartheid activist Steve Biko [who was beaten to death in prison].

Kipling was blanked (literally) not triggered. But what is relevant to the content warning issue is the seizure of cultural power and initiative by the student, not the staff, body. The act of enlightened obliteration was – to use a truly imperial metaphor – a shot across the university curriculum. It had its effect. The English course brochure description stresses the postcoloniality (anti-coloniality, it usually means) of the texts and critical theory studied nowadays in the English department. Out with Kipling; in with Fanon.

The distinguished historian of Britain and race David Olusoga was appointed as a professor at Manchester University a few months after the student protest. One of Britain's foremost public intellectuals, Professor Olusoga has been an eloquent critic not merely of Kipling but the Kiplingesque view of the

British Empire. Olusoga was offered, accepted and awarded OBE ('Officer of the Most Excellent Order of the British
Empire') by the Queen in 2019. I assume that, as a contrarian,
he agrees with George Bernard Shaw. As the Irish dramatist
demonstrated, in plays like *John Bull's Other Island*, the only
way to get through to Mr Bull is not by pointing out the obvious (he has raw beef between his ears) but by making fun of
him and the British Empire of which he's so fond.

ENID BLYTON: PARTIALLY DEPLAQUED, WHOLLY DEMINTED

Children's literature which acquires the status of 'beloved' has
a multigenerational bedtime life. Parents nostalgically buy
books (*Where the Wild Things Are, The Very Hungry Cater-
pillar, The BFG*) which delighted them for their own children.
The downside is that the world, and its sore points, change
with the generations and the passed-on beloved classics can be
an awkward fit. Too awkward sometimes for trigger warnings.

Homerton College, Cambridge, has one of the largest collections of children's literature outside the copyright libraries
(which have not, historically, been assiduous in collecting juvenile reading matter). As the student journal *Varsity* reported
in October 2021, Homerton had embarked on a project entitled 'Decolonising Digital Childhoods' intended to 'pilot techniques for diversifying digital access to and content within
archives of childhood'.

The project would focus on material held at Homerton in
collaboration with a similarly large collection in the Baldwin

Library of Historical Children's Literature at the University of Florida. The American side was supported by the University of Florida and a grant from the National Endowment for the Humanities. The joint aim was to 'prioritise the online provision of children's books by "people of colour" and texts that "showcase diversity"'. In order to go drag classic children's texts into the twenty-first century, a necessary degree of 'modernising' (i.e. meddling with the text) was foreseen. Some books, it was inferred but not stated outright, might find themselves in the poison cabinet. Protocols for deselection would be established.

The investigators Zoe Jaques and Eugene Giddens declared, in the manner of a papal bull, that Homerton's aim was to create a digital, online collection which would be 'less harmful in the context of a canonical literary heritage that is shaped by, and continues, a history of oppression ... It is a dereliction of our duty as gatekeepers to allow such casual racism [in children's literature] to go unchecked.'

The oppression alluded to was colonial in Britain, and in America, slavery and its legacy.

On the British side, the project, which received an £80,633 grant from the Arts and Humanities Research Council, is aimed to culminate with an online set of twenty children's books 'designed to explicitly engage with decolonising historical children's literature'. More generally, there would be 'trigger warnings, with indications of harmful content for intersectional identities, [which] will protect researchers, children, and general readers from offensiveness or hurt that can emerge in otherwise safe search queries or acts of browsing'.

Bubble wrap for Little Red Riding Hood.

The *Daily Mail* picked it up and blew it up. In the process, it gave examples. Laura Ingalls Wilder's *Little House on the Prairie* would be indicted for its 'stereotypical depictions of Native Americans': no longer 'Indians' and no longer 'redskins'. Dr Theodor Seuss Geisel, author of the Dr Seuss books, had perpetrated 'overt blackface'. Delving far back, Charles Kingsley's *The Water Babies* (1863) was warned about for derogatory comments about the Irish. The examples given were a long overdue draining of children's literature's cesspits. As perceived by a scrupulous sniff test. Whether they would use Inclusive Minds' eight-year-old 'inclusion ambassadors' was not recorded.

The drainage was taking place on other fronts. On 17 June 2021, English Heritage, a charity which cares for 400 or more British monuments and buildings, updated its website to note that Enid Blyton's children's books had 'uncomfortable aspects'. Action was called for:

> English Heritage unveiled a blue plaque to Enid Blyton in 1997 at her home in Chessington where the children's author – beloved by many – lived between 1920 and 1924. We updated our online Blyton entry in July 2020 and at the end of that entry, it includes a reference to the fact that the author's work has been criticised for its racism.

The charity added that it had no intention of tearing down its own plaques but would update its website with whatever triggering was necessary. It was impossible to do in situ; 'we can fit about 19 words on each plaque. Our website provides a fuller picture of the person's life, including any uncomfortable aspects.'

Apropos Blyton, the English Heritage website states: 'Blyton's work has been criticised during her lifetime and after for its racism, xenophobia and lack of literary merit.' It was felt too 'uncomfortable' to specify exactly what those wispy terms meant. The plaque stood – now an English Heritage monument to English pusillanimity about England's colonial heritage and Enid Blyton's utter disgracefulness.

English Heritage had been late in getting its plaques in order. With the turn of the centuries, there had been nervous signs that the tide was turning. As late as 2005, Pollock's Toy Museum, in central London, displayed, for sale, a magnificent display of golliwogs.

In April 2023, as recorded above, a squad of five policemen descended the White Hart Inn, a family-owned pub in Grays, Essex, to seize a collection of fifteen golliwog dolls, on shelf display above the counter. A hate crime was suspected.

Golliwogs were by now not, as they had been for a hundred years, a favourite little girls' doll, along with the teddy bear. The teddy itself warrants a parenthetic historical digression. It is named in honour of President Teddy Roosevelt, a ferocious hunter of wild animals (particularly American bears – some of whose subspecies, such as that emblazoned on the California state flag, are now extinct). Teddy Roosevelt is a patriarch of the National Rifle Association. His animal-slaughtering firearms are on display in the NRA museum. Sacred relics. The first Teddy Bears, commemorating his ursicide, were invented and went on sale in 1902, his first year in presidential office.

In twentieth-century Britain, the golliwog had been universalised not just in children's bedrooms but on the kitchen tables of working-class Britain by Robertson's, the maker of fine British jams, which used 'Golly' as its label mascot.

Robertson's had adopted the figure in the Edwardian period. It proved a brilliant marketing stroke. The golliwog brand-marked the product and, in 1928, inspired a spin-off campaign. In return for tokens from the jam pot, kids could get golly brooches and badges. The slump-ridden 1930s was the decade of the jam-sandwich supper. (Scrumptious when you considered the alternative: bread and dripping.) Children collected gollies as avidly as their descendants would Star Wars figures.

In 1961 there occurred what is called the 'Great Yellow Golliwog Panic'. It is described by Professor Lesley Hall of UCL and the Wellcome Institute:

In the summer of 1961 there was a panic about schoolgirls wearing yellow golliwogs as badges, which had *sinister import*. This first appears to have surfaced in a speech at the British Medical Association Annual Representative Meeting, 17 July 1961, by Dr R. G. Gibson, a member of Council, who averred that 'at a girls' school in England' (unnamed and not more specifically located, no indication of who might have been his informant) a yellow golliwog pinned to a girl's chest 'indicated to [her] fellow pupils that [she] had lost [her] virginity'. And this was a sign of the loss of moral discipline that was sweeping the country ... This was quite immediately taken up by the press – e.g. 'Doctors discuss loose living: Moral Problem of the Yellow Golliwogs', *Birmingham Post* ... and a question raised in Parliament [by William Hamilton]:

'The newspapers this morning contained a terrible indictment of the kind of society in which we live. Girls in one of our schools are now putting yellow golliwogs on their tunics to show that they have lost their virginity.'

The *Sunday Times* announced, on 8 December 1961, 'a searching and enlightening enquiry' entitled 'Your Teenage Daughter: Dilemma of the Middle-Class Parent', which began with reference invoking 'the much publicized yellow golliwog on the gym-slip ... a sad little badge of non-chastity among young British schoolgirls'. Two years later, Mary Quant would introduce the decade-defining miniskirt: more angst for the 'middle-class parent'.

As regards yellow golliwogs, the problem was, scour the schools of Britain as they might, no reporter could find an actual example of 'unchaste' girls sporting yellow golliwogs. Nor did any teacher report the practice. Truth is it never happened.

Robertson's weathered the 1961 storm (despite its being the maligned yellow badge) and, it being the swinging decade, the company might even have got a boost from it. But in the early 2000s, sensing less tractable trouble ahead, Robertson's retired Golly.

Who, though, invented the 'gollywog'? According to Robertson's commercial mythology, it was them. The British press dutifully parroted the firm's 2000 press release: 'Golly was discovered by John Robertson during a business trip to America in 1910. He noticed children playing with a rag doll made from their mother's black skirts and white blouses and thought he could use the idea to sell his product.'

According to Robertson's, wholly untruthful, version, 'gollywog' was an infantile mispronunciation of 'dolly-wolly'. The golliwog was actually the brainchild of two English ladies: Bertha Upton and her daughter Florence. The Upton family emigrated to America in 1870 and returned to England (penniless) when Mr Upton died, fifteen years later. In 1895, the Upton ladies enterprisingly wrote a children's book, *The Adventures of Two Dutch Dolls*. Bertha did the text, Florence the illustrations. The hero was 'Golliwogg' (*sic*) – a lovable (if hideous) 'pickaninny' (a word the ladies picked up in the US). 'Golliwogg' was inspired by a minstrel rag doll which Florence had played with as a child in New York. Its origin was in blackface minstrelsy.

The Adventures of Two Dutch Dolls was hugely successful. A dozen sequels had been published in England by 1909 – the year before John Robertson went to America. The venerable London firm, Longmans, published the Uptons' works.

Gollies were, in the early 1900s, all the rage in the nurseries of England. Making rag dolls out of discarded mourning garb was easy work in an age when every mother's hand held a sewing needle. Toy manufacturers jumped on the bandwagon.

There was a sideline industry in sewing patterns. Neither Upton nor Longmans had secured the copyright. It was in the public domain. Florence Upton died in 1922 (aged forty-nine). Her tombstone, in Hampstead Cemetery, bears the inscription: 'Creator of the Famous Gollywog'.

Generations of Britons grew up 'owning' gollies and loving them. After the Uptons' books faded from the scene, enter Enid Blyton, in the 1940s, with her series of stories, featuring the trio of tar-babies, the three golliwogs: 'Golly, Woggie, and Nigger'.

The Enid Blyton Society is a vigorous body with highly informed chat about its venerated author on its website. *The Three Golliwogs* is, in the 2000s, something of a thorn in its side. Take, for example, this knowledgeable but rueful post by Tony Summerfield, from 22 May 2006:

> The PC brigade latched onto [*The Three Golliwogs*] many years ago, it was one of the first books to be changed. The last edition that featured Golly, Woggie and Nigger was the Dean edition with a dustwrapper published in 1968 [the year of Blyton's death]. When it came out with a laminated cover in 1970 the names had already been changed to Waggie, Wiggie and Wollie (and these are the editions that are mostly offered on ebay). The next edition was the scarce Piccolo paperback in 1973 which also used these names.
>
> The final edition of the book, which had already had its

name changed to *The Three Gollies* was published as No. 18 in Dean's Reward Series in 1987. In 1992 a new No. 18 appeared, *The Children at Green Meadows*. The book was then rewritten and eventually republished by Award in 1994 with the title *Three Bold Pixies*.

As late as 1966, two years before her death, Enid Blyton published *The Little Black Doll*. It is, in the historical context, gobsmackingly awful. The titular doll, Sambo, is hated by all the white dolls and their white male homeowner. Sambo runs away from home and, by good luck, a rainstorm falls and washes away his 'ugly black face'. Now clean and pink faced, he returns home and is welcomed by all, owner and doll, as one of them. This, recall, is 1966: the Windrush immigration was at its height. The empire fallen, Britain was, grudgingly gradually, becoming multicultural (seventy-five years for the first Windrush invitees).* But not Enid.

Blyton presents a huge problem culturally because her writing and sales are monumental. She has sold more copies than any other children's writer in history with 700 titles and 600 million sales – overwhelmingly in Britain. Why not, then, erect a monument to her? One would hope the answer is obvious. Sadly, it seems it isn't.

The dilemma memorialising would represent (even though she was still a superseller) was demonstrated in 2018. For two years, the Royal Mint debated whether, as an act of national

---

* The Caribbean immigrants were recruited to fill labour shortages in the home market.

commemoration, to put this supremely British writer on a British 50p coin. This to be issued fifty years after her death in 1968.

She had never been nationally honoured. Agatha Christie, the creator of Poirot, was appointed a dame in 1971, but there was nothing of that kind for the creator of Noddy. Following the opinion of its advisory committee, the Royal Mint, after much likely headscratching, decided against a commemorative Blyton coin. Let her be forgotten.

A *Mail on Sunday*'s FOI request discovered that the reason was that bluntly: '[Blyton] is known to have been a racist, sexist, homophobe and not a very well-regarded writer'. Not very well regarded 600 million times, her defenders would say. Nonetheless, Homerton's poison cabinet awaits the arrival of *Noddy* and the *Famous Five*.

THE CRUCIFIXION: TOO PAINFUL?

In 2016, theology students enrolled for Glasgow University's 'Creation to Apocalypse: Introduction to the Bible (Level 1)' class were forewarned – by triggering – that the course, particularly a lecture on 'Jesus and Cinema', would contain 'graphic scenes of the crucifixion'. The warning was given well in advance so that students could skip the class without penalty. There is no record how many did do a bunk.

The *Daily Mail* went to town on it on 5 January 2017. Its article would be first in what would be a long trail of 'shock and horror' exposures about the nonsense, namely 'triggering', that British universities were up to. The Glasgow article was the declaration of the *Mail* group's 'war on woke'. The war-reporting proved excellent copy.

Triggering on this course for these Glasgow students was, it could be argued, responsibly pastoral. Particularly, that is, in a theological class in which members might have vocational hope of ordination and a life devoted to Christian service. Self-harming, as an act of devotional self-mortification of the flesh, might have been a health and safety concern.

The four accounts in the New Testament of the crucifixion are, in the King James Version, inspiringly beautiful literature. One need not be Christian to appreciate them. Films (the seminar topic, recall, is 'Jesus and the Cinema') are something else. To use Anthony Burgess's definition, films are kinetic not static. As in pornography, the moving visual image is more arousing (including aroused disgust) than black phonemes on a white surface.

Renaissance art is sometimes confusing in its making the appalling agony of Christ beautiful. Emulous almost. The subject is no longer widespread among major twentieth-century artists. But down the road from Glasgow University, in the Kelvingrove Art Gallery and Museum, is the ever-perverse Salvador Dali picture of the crucifixion. It shows, from above (a God's-eye view) a beautifully unhurt Christ, serenely on his cross, looking down on a placid lake. An analogous depiction is shown in Serrano's 'Piss Christ' – a beautiful, unblemished, Christ immersed in a flask of the artist's urine, washing away the agony.

From Cecil B. DeMille's silent *King of Kings* (1927) onwards, there have been twenty or more easily accessible film treatments of the Pathos of the Cross. The course designers at Glasgow would, I think, have had five, of high artistic distinction, in mind. They are, in order of popularity (i.e. box office receipt: one title is left out to be discussed later):

- Martin Scorsese: *The Last Temptation of Christ* (1988)
- Norman Jewison: *Jesus Christ Superstar* (1973)
- David Lean, Jean Negulesco, George Stevens: *The Greatest Story Ever Told* (1965)
- Paolo Pasolini: *The Gospel According to St Matthew* (1964)

All these were successful in revenue and review. All were in their different ways tactful, verging on reverent, about the sacrificial murder of Jesus. They tended to confirm (with the possible exception of Pasolini's Italianisation) rather than challenge belief among believers. They would, one thinks, supply relatively undisturbing seminars for those familiar with the gospel narratives and not possessed of overstrung nerves.

All four of them, however, were topped, financially, by the fifth film (left out of the above list), which cost pennies to make and which is in the highest degree challenging: traumatically so for some viewers.

It was, self-evidently, Mel Gibson's *The Passion of the Christ* (2004) which led the course committee at Glasgow to issue a trigger. There are a range of things in the film which render it a hard watch. Mel Gibson, actor and producer, is a connoisseur of masochism. In *Brave Heart*, as William Wallace, for example, he is, in character, half hung, stretched while still living on the rack, his disembowelled entrails burned in front of his dying face.

Gibson's depiction, as director, of the last twelve hours of Christ would be sadistic were it not so clearly devotional and literal. Voyeurism was, nonetheless, inevitable. The grisly scenes of the scourging and crucifixion in *The Passion* are available, free of charge, on YouTube for stop-start repeated contemplation. If, that is, you can bear the close-up depicted pain. Many can: the site has been visited by millions – not all, one suspects, in reverent search. The film was nominated for an Oscar for make-up. That is not, to Gibson's credit or discredit, what it looks like on screen, large or small. Without its creator wanting it, *The Passion* has become, on its darkest fringes, religioporn.

Another problematic aspect is that Gibson stresses over and again that the Jews, not the Romans, were to blame. The American Anti-Defamation League, after being invited by Gibson to a private viewing, issued a dignified denunciation:

ADL and its representatives have never accused Mr Gibson of being an anti-Semite. We do not know what is in his heart. We only know what he has put on the movie screen. The images there show Romans who behave with compassion toward Jesus. The Roman governor, Pontius Pilate, constantly expresses his reticence to harm Jesus. The Jews, on the other hand, are depicted as blood-thirsty. The Jewish

High Priest, Caiaphas, is shown as bullying Pilate, and the hundreds and hundreds of amassed Jews demanding Jesus' death.

As anti-Semitism increases around the globe, many are using the age-old deicide charge to legitimize and foment hatred against Jews.

One critic went so far as to call *The Passion* a Jew-hating snuff movie.

Gibson complicated his defence (which he politely but vigorously made to the ADL) by his behaviour when he was arrested on a drunk-driving charge on the road back from a bar to his home in Malibu two years after *The Passion*'s release. When detained, he turned to an arresting officer to say: 'Fucking Jews. The Jews are responsible for all the wars in the world. Are you a Jew?' After this lapse and rehab Gibson has been, it is authoritatively reported, sober.

Mel Gibson is, one can plausibly surmise, a deeply Christian man – but of an idiosyncratic kind, even for southern California. He was brought up, with his many brothers (by birth), a Sedevacantist Catholic. The papal throne is, for this tiny sect, empty and has been since Pope John XXIII, after his accession in 1963. John XXIII made his mission reconciliation between the Catholic Church and Judaism.

The ecumenicism and modernism of Pope John Paul II is for the Gibsons – Mel and his father Hutton Gibson – heresy. Mel reportedly called John Paul II 'the anti-Christ' and 'the devil'. A screenwriter who worked with him, Joe Eszterhas, alleges those remarks were made on set. Mel has, reportedly, endowed his own small Sedevacantist church.

Over the past decade, Mel Gibson has, according to friends, mended his ways and moderated his outbursts. His father Hutton, who died aged 101 in May 2020, was outspoken to the end. A few days before the release of his son's movie in 2004, Hutton insisted in a radio interview (picked up by the national networks) that the Holocaust was 'fiction': 'They claimed that there were 6.2 million [Jews] in Poland before the war and after the war there were 200,000, therefore [Hitler] must have killed 6 million of them. They simply got up and left. They were all over the Bronx and Brooklyn and Sydney and Los Angeles.'

In a network interview a few days later with Diane Sawyer, Mel Gibson declared his father was 'a man of truth … I'm tight with him. He's my father. Gotta leave it alone, Diane. Gotta leave it alone.'

How much the Gibson doctrines, *père et fils*, are present in *The Passion of the Christ* is a matter of dispute. The story of the film's conception, creation and distribution for cineastes is factual. It was not an easy birth. As a pitch, it was totally un-bankable from normal Hollywood studio sources. The script is in three languages, two of them dead: Hebrew, Latin and reconstructed Aramaic.

Gibson was initially against subtitles but eventually relented. Foreign-language subtitles are, usually, poison in Hollywood. The cast, for reasons of economy, were relatively unknown, with no audience pull. Gibson, enriched by his years as one of Hollywood's most bankable stars and wholly reliable on set, put together his own firm, Icon Productions. He scraped up a starter sum of $30 million for production costs – chump change in Hollywood terms. But spread thin, it was enough for him to get a cast, a crew and to cover filming expenses in Italy.

Getting the finished film out to paying spectators required ingenuity not thrift. It was unrateable on the normal PG and up scale. Given the violence, the MPAA would have ranked it triple X. Normal cinema circuits were blocked. The first version of the film was released to art houses and independent outlets.

It had, if anything, too great an impact. Gibson cut five minutes of the most intense depicted 'passion' (i.e. suffering) for a secondary version released in March 2005. His reasons were not mercantile but those of the proselytising preacher:

> After the initial run in movie theaters, I received numerous letters from people all across the country. Many told me they wanted to share the experience with loved ones but were concerned that the harsher images of the film would be too intense for them to bear. In light of this I decided to re-edit *The Passion of the Christ*.

What he meant by this was that like churches on Sunday, he wanted all family attendance. He was thinking congregations not audiences. He devised a hugely profitable film arterial distribution through churches which bought the film, as video, not just for showing in church halls but for their flock to buy.

The *Passion* was particularly congenial with Pentecostalists, Adventists, Christian Rapturists and other non-conformist denominations. If *The Passion* was religioporn on YouTube, it was gospel in churches. The revenues were eventually mountainous. The film grossed over $600 million in its first year. It is, two decades on, the most profitable Christian film ever. Gibson, reportedly, is making a sequel.

There is never anything clear-cut about Mel Gibson. He defies definition. So too his film. Glasgow's trigger warnings were cautious but, in my opinion, wholly justified.

GENDER QUEER: BEWARE!

The most banned book in America by several surveys in 2021 and 2022 was *Gender Queer: A Memoir*, by Maia Kobabe.[*] It may also qualify as the most triggered work in literary history so far. StoryGraph lists thirty-three ('user-submitted and author-approved') categories of serious warning (the bracketed numbers indicate intensity):

Dysphoria (133); Medical trauma (85); Blood (78); Sexual content (58); Medical content (56); Transphobia (37); Homophobia (13); Body horror (11); Deadnaming (10); Vomit (9); Body shaming (6); Panic attacks/disorders (6); Biphobia (4); Misogyny (4); Excrement (4); Outing (4); Bullying (3); Acephobia/Arophobia (3); Injury/injury detail (3);

---

[*] Banning as measured by public libraries and schools and by some state-wide listed mandates – Texas and Florida notably.

Lesbophobia (2); Toxic friendship (2); Adult/minor relationship (1); Alcoholism (1); Cancer (1); Cursing (1); Incest (1); Mental illness (1); Pedophilia (1); Rape (1); Self harm (1); Sexual violence (1); Grief (1); Pregnancy (1)

There are as many or more in the 'moderate' and 'minor' triggerable listings. The book carries a lot of critical weight.

Kobabe was born in 1989 and raised in Sonoma, southern California, 'out in the cow fields'. The Kobabes were a two-parent, biologically differentiated family. As Maia recalls:

Growing up in nature, I felt so safe and free to wander around the hillsides and talk to myself ... It was a very relaxed and natural childhood. I had space to be me, whatever that was, without being observed or judged or commented on by anyone. Every child should be so lucky.

The Kobabe seniors were 'benevolently hands off' and let Maia 'grow in my own shape'.

A crisis in that shape came with menstruation. It was felt as bodily betrayal by the eleven-year-old. Depression and dysmorphia ensued. Maia moved to the next serial transformations arriving at 'gender queer', non-binary, while attending university and the California College of the Arts in San Francisco.

Gender Queer: A Memoir, published in 2019, began as juvenile journaling. The first print version came out as graphic fiction, from Lion Forge comics. It was later picked up by Oni Press, with whom it became a superseller.

Kobabe is profoundly dyslexic and primarily thinks visually and identifies professionally as a cartoonist. I will borrow as general description a StoryGraph description of *Gender Queer*:

In 2014, Maia Kobabe, who uses e/em/eir pronouns, thought that a comic of reading statistics would be the last autobiographical comic e would ever write. At the time, it was the only thing e felt comfortable with strangers knowing about em. Now, *Gender Queer* is here. Maia's intensely cathartic autobiography charts eir journey of self-identity, which includes the mortification and confusion of adolescent crushes, grappling with how to come out to family and society, bonding with friends over erotic gay fanfiction, and facing the trauma and fundamental violation of pap smears.

Started as a way to explain to eir family what it means to be nonbinary and asexual, *Gender Queer* is more than a personal story: it is a useful and touching guide on gender identity – what it means and how to think about it – for advocates, friends, and humans everywhere.

In 2021, *Gender Queer* had become the most challenged book in the country, with objectors describing its candid discussion of gender fluidity as downright 'pornographic'. In an op-ed at the *Washington Post*, Kobabe movingly defended the vitality of books like *Gender Queer*, writing:

Queer youth are often forced to look outside their own homes, and outside the education system, to find information on who they are. Removing or restricting queer books in libraries and schools is like cutting a lifeline for queer youth, who might not yet even know what terms to ask Google to find out more about their own identities, bodies and health.

When asked about pronouns, Kobabe said: 'The ones I chose feel like a coat that fits.' That usage is called, in witness of its origin, 'Spivak'. Michael David Spivak was a mathematician specialising in 'differentialism'. It can be seen as a term with social as well as mathematical-geometric-algebraic application. Spivak, following this theme, introduced his gender-neutral pronouns in his book *The Joy of TeX*. TeX is a typesetting program which authors can use, closing the differential splits between writer, editor, typesetter, printer.[*]

Time magazine, in its review of *Gender Queer*, received a chorus of criticism for observing Kobabe's Spivak usage. To most it will seem mere courtesy.

The original comic book version of Kobabe's memoir would have come and soon gone in the normal churn of that genre. But young people more readily read comics than hardbacks. There is also vigorous word of mouth on social media. A month or two after publication, *Gender Queer* was noticed by adult custodians and began to be banned or remotely shelved by school boards, made up largely of parents.

The reason generally given was that it was pornographic.

---

[*] I like others have written books in TeX – liberating myself from the chores of text proofing, and publisher-imposed choice of font. This is not so typeset.

Looking back, Kobabe told *Slate* magazine: 'What I'm learning is that a book challenge is like a community attacking itself.' Kobabe's book had swirled to wide public notice in what e called 'a viral social media moment'. Confusion was a driving force: 'I want people to be confused about my gender at all times,' e has said.

Gender Queer – as the StoryGraph trigger categorisation and numerology makes clear – contains much pain. A quarter of the book ruminates on Kobabe's digital and physicians' specular investigations and invasions of eir insides. Kobabe resorts to illustration, not to print, in making eir point. Hence the 'pornography' canard.

The website 'Merry Misandrist' describes these awkwardly uncertain moments in Kobabe's becoming – to borrow Michelle Obama's term:

Kobabe goes to school and generally starts to realize that e may be gay. Kobabe also describes not exactly feeling comfortable as a woman but stops just short of identifying as a man. Kobabe wants to get rid of eir breasts and have top surgery, but what e desperately wants most of all is a penis. E hates getting pap smears and describes unbelievable pain as a result of the doctor using a speculum on em.

Banning makes readers curious, and curiosity means sales. Six-figure advances were reportedly offered for what Kobabe calls a 'next big book', to be published by Scholastic's imprint Graphix. It is provisionally entitled *Saachi's Stories*, by Maia

Kobabe and Lucky Srikumar. It is forecast for issue in spring 2025. Will *Gender Queer* have burned out by then? Or will it prove to be the pebble that starts an avalanche? Ron DeSantis, see below, is looking for his hard hat.

THE 47TH PRESIDENT?

Ron DeSantis had a problem. Governor of Florida since 2019 and a righter-than-right Republican, he, and his supporters, yearned for more than gubernatorial power. The Oval Office, no less. Standing in his way was an obstacle – not POTUS Joe Biden but ex-POTUS Donald Trump.

In the public mind, DeSantis had made his name as mini-Trump, not a rival. Politically, they were joined at the hip. Trump had a rock-hard, multistate, 'The Don or Die' constituency. No one would have stormed the Capitol (to hell with democratic institutions!) for Governor Ron DeSantis. Trump's electoral legions were vast: 70 million Americans at their height. Moreover, even in what some impertinently took as his senescence, he could rally a crowd and bully-pulpit his intraparty wannabes (the image of him looming, like a vengeful Nosferatu, behind Hillary at the candidate debate was indelible). He could use the microphone – studio or rally – like a conductor's baton (or baseball bat).

DeSantis was a wooden public speaker. But – and this counted among Republicans – he was younger, a proven winner (in Florida), a family man (no Stormy Daniels in Ron's wardrobe), a decorated soldier and, most importantly, 'not Trump'. He had a better chance of winning over the 'undecided' voter bloc on the 'not as bad as the other guy' calculus. And, unlike Trump, there was distance between him and the Q-Anon fanatic wing which terrified middle-class independent voters of all ethnicities.

But how could he topple Trump? Electioneering gets going early in the US. DeSantis began mobilising in early 2022. He was self-declared pro-life, actively supportive of immigrant deportation and sceptical that Covid-19 was as serious as the scientists said it was (what did they know) and had an 'A+ rating' from the National Rifle Association. His boxes had all the ticks.

He added to them with two wedge issues which would mark him as 'not Trump'. He was a law graduate from Yale and Harvard, sharpened by uniformed years in military intelligence. His first differentiating line of attack was CRT – critical race theory.

The theory argued that racism, even in America's post-egalitarian and post-Civil Rights Act society, was an ingrained thing in the privileged (overwhelmingly non-black) majority. After racism's scabs were ripped off in 1964, it remained a virus in the body of America – something you could not see other than by its effects and the structures it erected.

America, DeSantis proclaimed, was being brainwashed by CRT hogwash. The enemy was, in the word of the day, the 'woke': the *soi-disant* 'enlightened' elite. Pointy-headed professors who had difficulty parking their bicycles straight. He launched his anti-CRT campaign in mid-2021. The response was encouraging. At the end of the year, he introduced his Stop Woke bill: 'Stop Wrongs to Our Kids and Employees'. The principal wrong was educational instruction that teaches that individuals are 'inherently racist, sexist, or oppressive, whether consciously or *unconsciously*'.* In promoting the bill, he proclaimed: 'No taxpayer dollars should be used to teach our kids to hate our country or hate each other.'

The bill ran into problems in the courts, but it elevated the governor's standing as Florida's white saviour. PEN America recorded 566 books banned in state schools in the 2021–22 school year. They were banned on the sole authority of Florida's governmental-appointed inspectors. No appeal allowed.

DeSantis followed the Stop Woke bill with policy initiatives popularly referred to as 'Don't Say Gay'. It was a historic back-hander at Bill Clinton's rule about gay people in the military, DADT – don't ask, don't tell. Well, Ron DeSantis (no draft dodger he) would tell it straight.

The eventual bill was entitled 'Parental Rights in Education'. It would ban public schoolteachers in Florida from mentioning sexual orientation or gender identity from kindergarten through third grade. The hope was to enlarge the prohibition to twelfth grade. This duly happened in April 2023.

To get the bill off the ground, DeSantis held a press conference in Tampa on 8 March 2023 with a large sympathetic

---

* My stress.

non-journalistic audience in attendance. It was an unusual event, as such things go. It was 'triggered'.

The event revolved around a six-minute video. A handout warned that the video would display 'material that is sexually explicit in nature and not suitable for children'. Or, as it happened, for network TV. They were forewarned and duly made arrangements and cut their live feeds at strategic points. In a devious way, DeSantis could be thought to be breaking his own law – he was trafficking porn (as he defined it).

Graphic books for children were the target. Topping the *Index Librorum Prohibitorum Floridiensum* (DeSantis called it 'garbage') was, inevitably, *Gender Queer* along with Mike Curato's *Flamer*, another graphic narrative, showing Boy Scouts at summer camp teaching each other how to masturbate. Significantly, among the illustrations was a portrayal of sexual acts between a black and a white Scout. The faintest echo of that old KKK slogan word 'miscegenation' could be heard. Also displayed were graphic panels from *This Book Is Gay*, a manual for those accommodating to gay existence and practices. Pictures from *Let's Talk About It*, a book with illustrated advice on masturbation and sexting, was screened. It was a lively six minutes and can be visited on YouTube. DeSantis's killer punch was the report that many in Hollywood opposed his bill. 'If the people who held Harvey Weinstein up oppose us on parents' rights, I wear that like a badge of honor,' he breast-thumpingly threw back.

DeSantis now had his contre-Trump issue armed and was ready to go with it. But he also had his fifth column within his ranks: Walt Disney World – one of Florida's paramount tourist industries. Disney had some murky racially phobic twentieth-century history, but in the twenty-first century it was progressive verging on woke. The last thing it wanted was a gay boycott. Having quietly detached itself from any state tax sanctions, Disney World declared (culture) war on the governor's initiative with outright denunciation in March 2022:

> Florida's HB 1557, also known as the 'Don't Say Gay' bill, should never have passed and should never have been signed into law. Our goal as a company is for this law to be repealed by the legislature or struck down in the courts, and we remain committed to supporting the national and state organizations working to achieve that.

DeSantis responded by calling Disney's objection to his bill as 'fundamentally dishonest' and said he would not bow down to the California-based company.

On 17 April 2023, he took the fight to them: he would cut their preferential tax status ('We want to make sure that Disney lives under the same laws as everybody else'); introduce more frequent inspections of the safety of the rides and mono-rail; and, he thought, build a state prison on some state land alongside Disney World.

DeSantis's battles with Trump and Disney continue. The smart money is on Mickey and the percentage bets are on Trump. And Ron for POTUS? The polls, at time of writing, don't see it.

STIRLING UNIVERSITY DUMPS A COLONIAL RELIC

There were newspaper headlines in April 2022 – following the by-now familiar 'whatever next?' pattern – announcing that, shock-horror, 'Jane Austen [is] dropped from university's English course to "decolonise the curriculum"'.

The university doing the dropping was Stirling in Scotland. A 'Lit 101' module had removed to library access *Pride and Prejudice* to make room for Toni Morrison's *Beloved*: a novel about post-Civil War African Americans still haunted by slavery – a crime against humanity not abolished but modernised.

Stirling's banishment was, it initially announced, an act of 'curriculum decolonization'; a pedagogic mucking out of the literary stables. The university did not feel it necessary to talk up the Nobel Prize-winning Morrison. Her awards spoke for themselves.

Jane Austen's long journey from being the essence of English gentility to an avatar of whip-wielding imperial tyranny, a Simon Legree and Edward Colston in bonnets, is a long and bumpy narrative. One could build an interesting first-year course around the Jane Austen critical and reputational rollercoaster.

Miss Austen (how she would have hated 'Ms') wrote her early work (including the first draft of *Pride and Prejudice*, then called *First Impressions*) during the Napoleonic Wars: Austen's novel was published two years before the decisive battle of Waterloo. No author is, superficially, less a wartime novelist – although, when you look behind the novel's frontline dramatis personae, there's a lot of militiamen in uniform (Darcy and Bingley are late eighteenth-century draft dodgers). One of the militia officers serving the king against Boney, George Wickham (an utter rotter), swoops in to seduce and carry off fifteen-year-old Lydia Bennet. The soldier's way. The Battle of Waterloo was fought on the lawns of Longbourn.

For a few years after the 1811 appointment of the future George IV, Austen earned the epithet (with its hint of dress embonpoint) 'Regency' novelist. Biography certifies she had few of the vices of Byron's fat friend. She died, unmarried, sadly young, in 1817 – before the Prince Regent succeeded to the throne as George IV. *Pride and Prejudice* is nobly dedicated (not Jane's idea, scholars agree) as such: 'To His Royal Highness, The Prince Regent. This work is, by His Royal Highness's permission, most respectfully dedicated by His Royal Highness's dutiful and obedient humble servant, The Author.'

Her thoughts about 'Prinny' were anything but respectful. She detested him for his treatment of his wife, Caroline of Brunswick. In a letter of 1813, as the novel appeared, she wrote: 'Poor woman, I shall support her as long as I can, because she *is* a Woman, & because I hate her Husband.' He, it is recorded, had a high opinion of her fiction. He bought two copies of *Pride and Prejudice*.

Victorians largely saw Jane Austen as a pleasantly amusing 'novelist of manners' of no great weight – compared, say, to Walter Scott (whose name they did not yet know). On his part, the Wizard of the North had an unfashionably high opinion of her, hailing her as a 'domestic', teacups novelist, whereas the anonymous 'author of *Waverley*' was swinging claymores all the way.

Austen evidently concurred with the Great Unknown on the issue of domesticity. How on earth could she compete with 'men' writers, she asked her nephew, James Edward Austen-Leigh, who had authorial ambition and wanted a few tips: 'What should I do with your strong, manly, spirited Sketches, full of variety and Glow? How could I possibly join them on to the little bit (two inches wide) of Ivory on which I work with so fine a Brush, as produces little effect after much Labour?'

One wonders if young James caught the irony. Not everyone does or did with Miss Austen.

Where, though, did that two inches of notional ivory come from? Hairy mammoths had not run wild in Hampshire for 5,000 years. It was, in the nineteenth century, imported, raw or worked on, from the East India Company's domain and its workforce elephants. And what of the binding agent in Miss Austen's ink? It came from British trading posts in West Africa. Without pursuing metaphors into triviality (viz, the teacups 'interrogation', above), Jane Austen may have been, as she says, a miniaturist, but there were tiny filaments, in her act of writing, to what was becoming the biggest empire in history and sucking the world's wealth into its tiny windswept self. After, that is, Napoleon was put down.

Anticipating D. H. Lawrence's masculinist putdown 'narrow-gutted spinster' (by which he meant corseted and old-maid), Charlotte Brontë found the Austen world disgustingly over-civilised when, late in life, she first read *Pride and Prejudice*:

'What did I find? An accurate, daguerreotyped portrait of a commonplace face; a carefully fenced, highly cultivated garden, with neat borders and delicate flowers; but no glance of a bright, vivid physiognomy, no open country, no fresh air, no blue hill, no bonny beck.'

The Scotism 'bonny beck' is a deferential nod to Walter Scott who, as said, had a high estimate of Austen. Thackeray (whom Brontë adored) like Scott read Austen admiringly and borrowed her plot devices and aspired to her fine English and subtle ironies.* Many of those who knew fiction because they wrote it saw her discreet worth.

The Austen *oeuvre* sold moderately, generation after Victorian generation, mainly in budget-priced reprint series ('Standard Novels') forerunners of the 'paperback', pioneered by the enterprising publisher Henry Colburn, who bought them from the Austen estate and rights' owners for pennies and sold them to local circulating libraries for shillings. They filtered into the English soul decade in, decade out.

Trollope's robust declaration in his autobiography, in 1883, that Jane Austen was a novelist of major importance planted a landmark flag. She had, by the time Trollope hailed her, established her base with the common reader. It helped install her that no female author of standing (forget the Brontës with their bonny becks) was judged less likely to bring a blush to the maiden cheek. She was Mrs Grundy's first call as a writer for the family listening to papa read of an evening. She never

---

* I write about his tribute borrowings in *Is Heathcliff a Murderer?* (1996).

saw Scotland, Wales or abroad and rarely the sea. She was distilled Englishness.

The Jane Austen Society, formed in 1940, mobilised a corps of long-standing 'Janeites' (Rudyard Kipling's affectionate term) who reread the six great works every year as faithfully as they recited the Creed at matins every Sunday. One could be 'fond' in that way of Jane Austen but never 'fond' of, say, prickly Charles Dickens.

In the turbulent early twentieth century, Jane Austen routinely served as a national literary tranquilliser. She anchored something. When Orwell – writing in wartime – incarnated 'characteristic fragments of the English scene', the spirit of the country as (among many other things like knobbly faces, unarmed policemen, cricket and warm beer) the image of 'old maids biking to Holy Communion through the mists of the autumn mornings', what old maid's fiction comes to mind? Not George Eliot.

Austen's novels gave assurance that there was an England to save as its empire dripped away – at first slowly (with India), then climactically. Harold Macmillan, who oversaw actual 1950s decolonisation, a PM of the very oldest school, said that sometimes the strain of Downing Street was so great 'you have to resort to Jane Austen'. He gave that advice to Margaret Thatcher, who preferred naughty Jeffrey Archer. Supermac would roguishly quip he liked to go to bed with a Trollope.

The fact that there is no bodily sex in Austen's novels (she never wrote of things she did not know), nor French Revolution complication in the background, made her an eminently eligible choice in A-level exams which came into being in 1951 with the New Elizabethan era. *Emma* was a required text when I did my A-levels in 1955. Working class by background, I felt myself one of the huge unnamed mass on which the world of the Bennets and Darcys and Bingleys rested. The kind of person who mucked out the stables and aspired one day to be a footman. There are servants everywhere in Austen's fiction. The Austen world could not run without them. Can you think of a single servant's Christian name or surname? I can think of one – James, the coachman in *Emma*. There would have been half a dozen indoor servants, cooking, cleaning, washing in Hartfield. Nameless, faceless, attic 'dormers' to sleep in.

Martin Amis, writing in the libertine '60s, thought *Pride and Prejudice* a goodish novel – but it would be tops if Jane Austen had added twenty-four pages on the Darcys' wedding night. In his 1995 BBC TV adaptation, Andrew Davies rose to the Amis challenge. Surviving Janeites recoiled. But their idol survived sex, drugs and rock and roll thanks to a multitude of TV, radio and film adaptations. And A-levels. The nation took Jane Austen as they had taken cod-liver oil during wartime. Both 'did you good'.

Some critics, with the literary equivalent of the sonar devices designed to detect enemy submarines, insisted the reverberations of world events and sheer human nastiness were there in Austen's six great novels if you looked deep and cocked your ear sensitively enough.

In the '50s and onwards, Oxbridge 'dons' and 'fellows' (female scholars leading the way) pointed out uncosy things in the Austen plotwork. Under the conduct-manual carapace, neo-Freudian analysis could detect seething Freudian malevolence. Why did Elizabeth Bennet despise all her sisters bar one, Jane, who is said to be less intelligent than her? There was miasmic familial hatred in the Austen world, like the grit in the oyster producing its pearls.

It was with second-wave feminism in the 1960s and its connection with universities that scholarly interest in Jane Austen became Apollo-propelled. She was by the 1980s elevated, by now intense scholarly exegesis, into neo-Shakespearean status. No self-respecting English studies student, sixth-form pupil to MA postgraduate, should be without a touch of Austen in the curriculum.

No sex? Look again. What about her sharing a double bed with her sister, Cassandra (as does, presumably, Emma with her friend Harriet at Hartfield)? Austen preserved letters, but all intimate correspondence between her and her sister was destroyed. Jane Austen, an incestuous lesbian? Trollope where art thou? 'Was Jane Austen Gay?' yelled the *London Review of Books* on its front pages on 3 August 1995. Yes, was the answer in the air. Why had she turned down the only eminently suitable man who proposed to her? What of herself did she want to preserve from male invasion?

Marilyn Butler's *Jane Austen and the War of Ideas* (1975) was long-term influential in finding depths of political and social thought under the soil in Brontë's wrongly supposed miniaturist garden-fenced, small-minded life. Austen's was a large world contained within a small world.

As regards sexual politics, she was as the twentieth century drew to an end, no longer Macmillan's Valium pill but a thinker as razor-minded, and capable of taking on the tyrant sex and the patriarchal world, as Mary Wollstonecraft herself.

And yet, in April 2022, Jane Austen – a novelist with all these facets and obscure depths expressing herself, wittily, in the most beautiful English – had been dumped by Stirling University. Why? One could, with a world-weary sigh, argue that nothing lasts. There are no fixtures in the literary canon, no 'immortels' as the French, with typical *grandeur*, call the members of their *Académie française*: not even Shakespeare. Not even Shakespeare? Yes, indeed. See above his pulling down at UPenn – the Bardless curriculum was becoming a widespread phenomenon in the English-speaking and reading world.

There was another erosive force, mentioned several times above. The pedestal on which the late twentieth century had placed Jane Austen was crumbling in the twenty-first century. Recent research, with a Cromwellian decolonising mission, turned up hugely uncomfortable facts about the Austen family and its assumed country parson ethos.

Literary criticism had long been aware, and taken on board, that the bricks of the great house in Mansfield Park must have been stained with slave blood. The estate's munificence was substantially drawn from the Bertram family's sugar plantation in the Leeward Islands colony, Antigua. The novel's main narrative is, historically, between autumn 1810 and summer 1813. The novel was published in May 1814.

Revenue in the central plot of *Mansfield Park* is running short for the Bertrams. Constant slave dissidence – despite the whip, rape and torture to keep the black workforce in line – and Napoleon's stubborn refusal to be defeated, along with the War of 1812 with America, are responsible for Sir Thomas, his little dynasty and his estate facing hard times. None of these are mentioned directly but reverberate through the fabric of the narrative. For two core years of the novel's narrative, Sir Thomas is absent, seeing to his Antigua plantation. His son and heir, the utter wastrel, Thomas Jr, accompanies him.

Sir Thomas is, although the word is never used in the novel, a 'Plantocrat'; in Parliament he would be a member of the 'West Indies Interest' lobby. Pro-slavery to a man. It was also their 'interest' to keep the price of sugar (their Caribbean islands being Britain's main supplier) prohibitively high. For the common people of England, sugar was a luxury. Hence Jane Austen's key to the sugar cabinet at Chawton.

All proves well. The novel sighs, silently, with relief. Slavery, and with it the Bertram luxurious country house life, has been saved. Slaves in Antigua will be under the whip until the mid-1830s, before being 'indentured' into quasi-slavery. The novel's hero, Fanny, once she is married to Edmund, will live on in slave-earned wealth.

What the Bertrams, *père et fils*, actually do in Antigua to get their plantation in order is never described by Jane Austen. How could she know? A 1999 film of *Mansfield Park*, deeply indebted to Edward Said's scholarship (particularly *Culture and Imperialism*, 1993), departed from Austen's narrative to depict in snapshots the awful sado-sexual things Sir Thomas got up to on his plantation, where every black body was his private property. Work? Whip? Rape? Sell?

Most importantly, according to Edward Said, *Mansfield Park* and with it the whole of Austen's fiction promotes 'a domestic imperialist culture without which Britain's subsequent acquisition of territory would not have been possible'. It normalised, and accepted as God's will, that there should be slavery – whatever freethinking radicals thought.

Austen's pretty English garden (about which Charlotte Brontë is so snide) and the brutally slave-worked colonial sugar plantation are, in *Mansfield Park*, conjoined. That, of course, is fiction. But so, as it happens, were historical Antigua and the 'cottage' (actually a large house) in Chawton, Hampshire, where the Austens resided and Jane wrote her novels. As Hitler's bombs blitzed down on England, the Jane Austen Society was founded to save the building (and by implication England) from dilapidation. It now houses the Jane Austen's House Museum. It too (see above) is suffering the literary equivalent of woodworm.

The worms bore deep. Jane Austen's father, a clergyman in the established Church of England, had been at one time the principal trustee of an Antigua sugar plantation. He was so in the interest of one of his close friends (and the godfather of one of his male children), James Langford Nibbs. The Nibbses, a titled family, had been one of the island's main Plantocrats for three generations. The Revd George Austen knew all about what went on in Antigua, and so must his daughter have known. It seems from what slight evidence there is that Jane tended towards abolition. Whether with a pang of guilt as she dipped into the sugar bowl with her teaspoon is not recorded.

Stirling in 2022 faced a dilemma – decolonising Austen meant at least spending a big chunk of very limited seminar hours on predictably contentious discussion, much of which would be beside the point and tendentious. This was an introductory course, not a battleground. In the face of the furore its dropping *Pride and Prejudice* had whipped up – the *Daily Mail* leading the charge – Stirling backtracked with bland announcements and letters to the opinion-forming press. The 'removal', it explained, was initially taken in the interest of 'decolonising the curriculum' and 'diversity'; the issues it raised were 'racial difference and critical race theory, gender and sexuality'. Austen was inappropriate for this particular course because there was too much, not too little, in her.

But, it informed the press, Stirling's 'Special Authors Module changes focus on an annual basis and aims to introduce students to a diverse range of writers, including international voices and those from British literary history'.

As someone whose business was once upon a time composing curricula, I think Stirling's changing the first-year menu was understandable. But using the term 'decolonise' was bound to be provocative. Filleting state ideology out of a classic work of literature is a delicate operation, and what is left when you pin the winkle out of its shell? We murder to dissect, said Wordsworth – it should be engraved as a warning over the lintel of every door leading to the English department.

BUGGERY AND BESTIALITY: AT THE GLOBE?

Since its arrival on the cultural-educational scene around 2013, triggering had, ten years on, refined and redefined itself. Superficially, it is a defence mechanism for the post-traumatised, physically challenged, discriminated against and emotionally vulnerable.

But triggering and content warnings have another defensive role. They defend the provider as well as the recipient. How this works is best shown in a recent example of the kind of minuet with the consumer that triggering has become. In February 2023, the Globe Theatre – the reconstruction of Shakespeare's South Bank theatre (less the stench from the nearby bear-baiting ring) – announced that for its summer season (it being a summery play), it would be putting on a performance of *A Midsummer Night's Dream*. It would, as nowadays is common practice, be as unlike an actual performance of the Shakespearean age as it is possible to get while respecting the sanctity of the text.

Accompanying this production in the programme was a trigger warning: 'Content guidance: The play contains language of violence, sexual references, misogyny and racism.' Those 'concerned about the play's themes' should 'contact the ticketing team for further details on the play's content'. What's this 'ticketing team'? Wasn't it once upon a time called 'box office'?

'*A Midsummer Night's Dream* Goes Woke' was the *Mail* headline, harping on a now familiar string. The vacuity of the 'guidance' (not 'warning') tinkles. What specifically, in terms of 'enactment', is being red-flagged here? By locating it in 'language' not 'performance', the responsibility is shifted on to Shakespeare – who, unlike the ticketing team, was unable to respond and would probably have done so bluntly.

What, manifestly, the Globe management was doing here was covering their theatre's backside. They had caught a bad cold with international scorn for their over-the-top warnings on *Romeo and Juliet* in 2021 (see above). No more Samaritan phone numbers would be provided.

This protective vagueness – not saying outright what it meant – is probably the result of careful 'legalling'. Should any of the audience sue for post-traumatic or actual-traumatic stress, the theatre was 'covered' – it had issued a warning. *Caveat emptor*: you brought it on your own head.

The new Globe itself is a major triumph of two things: the vision, drive and decades-long lobbying by the American Shakespeare lover Sam Wanamaker; and British Shakespearian scholarship. There is, frustratingly, no surviving reliable pictorial record of what Shakespeare's theatre or even, authentically, Shakespeare's stage was like (proscenium? Picture framed?). The only hints within the plays themselves are about such things as windows, balconies, trapdoors and night-sky-painted canopies.

Archaeological reconstruction from the Rose Theatre further down the South Bank supplied some, but not authoritative, evidence about physical layout, and the interesting fact that the standing audience shelled and ate nuts while watching – conversely, popcorn is not available at either the old or the new Globe. Wardrobe inventories supplied valuable information. Elizabethan and Jacobean theatres went big on costume. But the simulacrum which the new Globe represents is constructed by the hypotheses of scholarship as much as with board, plank, beam plaster and paint.

A Midsummer Night's Dream, as all modern editions make clear, pivots on multiple imminent or threatened rapes. The first such, with which the play opens, is the celebration, in Athens, of the marriage of Theseus and Hippolyta. A public holiday has been declared. Theseus is a conquering king; Hippolyta a conquered Amazon warrior queen. Amazons are not women of the marrying kind. The marriage, and its consummation, will be enforced and non-consensual. *Droit de roi.*

The Titania and Oberon parody plot has a parallel situation: an unwilling woman coerced into sexual act. The play's main action takes place in a 'wood' outside Athens. Woods, nature unpacified by man, are where social and sexual constraints drop away – the word has a secondary meaning 'mad' and an echo of 'wooed'. The four young lovers who are central are, in the woods, drugged, by a potion dabbed on the eyes, into falling instantly and 'madly' in love with someone else.

There is a continual hint of 'improper' sexual consummation. It is a naughty play. The 'potion' is the Shakespearian version of Rohypnol. In the fairyland parody plot, Titania is also drugged into falling madly in love, and physical embrace, just this side of 'all the way', with one of the 'rude mechanicals' (i.e. working-class tradesmen) 'translated' (metamorphosed) into a donkey.* The question of whether the translation extends below the waist is teasingly left to the audience's imagination. Few don't imagine. Women forced into sex with donkeys, or asses, is a theme reaching back through the ages to Apuleius's *The Golden Ass*, in the second century. The text was translated into English in 1566. Shakespeare evidently knew it.

In the book *The Production of English Renaissance Culture*, Bruce Thomas Boehrer has a chapter frankly entitled 'Bestial Buggery in *A Midsummer Night's Dream*'.

Underneath its gaiety, and play with love of the eye, love of the heart and love of the loins, *A Midsummer Night's Dream* is, for those who vibrate to it, a deeply disturbing play.

The contemporary Globe – with its scholarly advisory 'team' – is up with all the critical exegesis, past and present, on one of the naughtiest (but frequently funniest) of Shake-speare's works. Needs must, the theatre must give a warning in this day and age if only to protect themselves: but 'audience guidance: this play contains bestial buggery and drug-rape'? Throw a bucket of verbal fog over that, otherwise it'll be the 2021 disaster all over again.

---

* The rude mechanicals' parody plot, Pyramus and Thisbe (as well as self-parody by Shake-speare against his own *Romeo and Juliet*), is derived from Ovid's *Metamorphoses*. In May 2015, students at Columbia University demanded that Ovid's *Metamorphoses*, a text in a Lit 101 'Western classic literature' course, have a trigger warning imposed for the rape and transgen-der issues that the work raises. The warning was duly imposed.

EPILOGUE

While writing this book, I find myself in a place (old age) in which one thinks about things; insofar as the power to think remains. Why did I spend fifty-five years of my working life reading, teaching and writing about literature? To quote Wordsworth again: 'Up, up and leave your books' – there's a real world out there, he tells us. Why, at the decisive moments in my life, did I not follow Wordsworth's advice?

The answer is obvious enough to me. Because, as a child, books were a world more real to me than the wartime and post-war England I had been born into. I've indulged myself with a memoir called *The Boy Who Loved Books*. It was my first love and longest lasting.

A child's love of literature has magic carpet transport about it. An example comes to mind. On 24 August 1806, Samuel Taylor Coleridge and Charles and Mary Lamb came to tea and supper with the philosopher William Godwin. Godwin's little daughter Mary (later Mary Shelley; her mother, Mary

Wollstonecraft, had died giving birth to her) heard Coleridge recite 'The Rime of the Ancient Mariner'.

Ever the overhearer of influential men, Mary hid behind a sofa to listen, invisibly. Coleridge, one fancies, never knew she was there. A few years later, having eloped with the poet Shelley, Mary wrote the first draft of *Frankenstein*: Coleridge's Gothic seed had sprouted to another Gothic masterpiece. Both works have been currently triggered.[*]

The first 'grown-up' book which transported six-year-old me out of my then dreary world was *The Wind in the Willows*. Alas, it did not plant a seed which grew into creative writing; but it set me on the path of becoming 'a louse on the locks of literature' – a critic. I had a recurrent area of interest: Victorian fiction. I wrote a cyclopaedia on it; not a magnum opus but the biggest thing I shall leave behind me.[†]

We shall never know the Victorians as well as they knew themselves, try as we do. Nor – however well we annotate our texts – can we read Victorian novels as in the same way as Victorians read them. They, not we, own their fiction. We visit it as we visit those National Trust houses described above.

I was born in 1938. Thirty years after Queen Victoria died, leaving behind her a world which was slow to change, clinging on to its disappearing empire. Historically I'm closer to Victoria Regina than Mrs Thatcher PM. She changed a lot.

I was raised largely by grandparents born in the late 1880s. They were 'decent' working class but functionally literate

---

[*] At Greenwich University and doubtless elsewhere.

[†] *The Longman Companion to Victorian Fiction* (1988, revised 2009).

thanks to Forster's 1870 universal education act. My earliest memories are of milk delivered by horse carts, streets paved with odoriferous creosote-soaked wooden blocks which sweated in summer, the lamplighter (always the same one) coming at dusk with his hooked and glowing pole to illumine the street lights (a gentler light than electricity); gaslights in houses going on at home a little later.

In a nearby street to my grandparents' artisans' terrace house was a blacksmiths. I never reread *Great Expectations* without nasal memory of that acrid smell of coke sweetened by the aroma of leather and horse droppings. It's the only shit that smells sweet, Orwell pointed out. I am not a Dickensian – although I have written books on the Inimitable and I write about him here. I've also written a book on Orwell on smell, stink, odour and fragrance. The 1940s and 1950s were an odoriferous world under the haze of cigarette smoke. I loved the 'peasoupers', which were gradually dissolved after the great smog of December 1952.

One Victorian author, above all, I have loved. William Makepeace Thackeray. I have written books on him, edited his major texts and churned out articles on him for learned journals. A labour of love. I still reread him (never my articles): I love the sound of his rich clubman prose rising off the page. I joined the Athenaeum briefly for one thing. To sit in the drawing room where, sometimes in the morning, sometimes after supper, by candlelight, he wrote *The History of Henry Esmond* using crested club paper.

But nowadays, in the third decade of the twenty-first

century, and my ninth decade, my love for Thackeray is shadowed – guilty at times; self-triggered, one might say.

Thackeray and his original readers shared a common ground so familiar that there was no need for it to be spelled out. The challenge for today's reader is to reconstruct that ground as fully as we can: if only as a map to direct us through the narrative. To 'Victorianise' ourselves.

When asked on *Desert Island Discs* (a strange experience) what book I would take, as the rest of my life's reading matter, to my island, I came up with *Vanity Fair*. Can we, 180 years after its publication, in reading Thackeray's masterwork, 'Victorianise' our contemporary sensitivities about – to take something much triggered nowadays – race? Or should we aggressively confront it? Read it with cold decolonising eye and pass by?

Race crops up in the opening pages of *Vanity Fair*. Thackeray's first full-page illustration (he did them himself) in the novel shows the coach carrying Amelia and Becky (she hurling her Dr Johnson's 'Dixonary' out of the window) from Miss Pinkerton's to the freedom of Russell Square. Free, free at last. Looked at closely, we may also note a black footman standing on his footplate at the back of the Sedley coach. The driver, cracking his whip, is white.

The black footman, we later learn, is called Sambo. It is not his name – but black people do not have the right to their own names. They are what their masters call them. Sambo features a couple of times in the first numbers as a below-stairs house servant and his presence hints, obliquely, that the slave trade is one field of business that the two rich merchants, Mr Sedley and Mr Osborne, will have made their fortunes in. The 'trade' (i.e. transporting) in slaves was, of course, abolished by Wilberforce's Act in 1807, but already-resident slaves continued to work, their offspring born into slavery, in the British West Indies on the sugar plantations until the 1830s. The opening chapters of *Vanity Fair* are set in 1813 in the run up to Waterloo.

When we first encounter George Osborne and William Dobbin, they are junior officers just back from the West Indies. What was their regiment doing? Victorian readers needed no informing. It was (to them) self-evident. They were protecting vital British interests in sugar cane production in the Caribbean possessions of the Crown.[*]

There is another character in the novel with an interest in the West Indies. Amelia's and Becky's schoolmate at Miss Pinkerton's academy, Miss Swartz, is introduced as the fabulously 'rich woolly-haired' mixed-ethnic pupil from St Kitts. St Kitts, like Antigua, is one of the Leeward Islands in the Caribbean and had (until well into the twentieth century) a monoculture economy based on one crop: sugar. The plantations were worked, until the mid-1830s, by slaves – of whom Miss Swartz's mother must have been one. Dobbin's and George's regiment, the '—th', has recently been garrisoned at St Kitts just before we encounter them. One of their duties would be to put down the slave rebellions. Brutally, if necessary; it often was.

---

[*]   For more on this, refer to the entry on Jane Austen above.

Miss Swartz is, we deduce, the daughter of a sugar Plantoc-rat (the surname hints at Jewish paternity, echoing the offen-sive Yiddish term '*schvartze*') who has consoled himself with black slave concubines. This was normal abusive practice. It was also something painfully familiar to Thackeray. His father had been a high-ranking official in the East India Company. William himself was born in Calcutta and educated in Eng-land's best schools and universities on 'nabob' wealth. Before marrying, Thackeray's father, as was normal, had a 'native' mistress and by her an illegitimate daughter, Sarah Blechyn-den. It was an embarrassment to the novelist, who declined any relationship with his half-sister all his life.

In the truly hideous depiction Thackeray made of Miss Swartz for Chapter 21 ('Miss Swartz Rehearsing for the Drawing-Room'), one may suspect spite and an element of shame. What was the abolitionist's motto – 'Am I not a Man and a Brother?' What was Miss Swartz's mute cry, 'Am I not a Woman and a Sister?' No, is the answer Thackeray's novel throws back. The Jewishness of Miss Swartz clearly provokes racism in Thackeray.

Vanity Fair was Thackeray's first full-length work of fiction. He lived sixteen more years and his views on race remained unreconstructed. One could argue they became more poi-soned, as did Dickens's, after the Indian Uprising.

In a letter sent to his mother from America, on a munificent lecturing tour, he wrote of the black slaves he saw in the south: 'They are not my men and brethren, these strange people with their retreating foreheads, and with great obtruding lips and jaws ... Sambo is not my man and my brother.'

Thackeray died in 1863 during the American Civil War. He had earlier proclaimed himself a firm supporter of the Confederacy and slavery. He had, he joked, thousands of good reasons for doing so – he had invested that many dollars in the slave-owning south via the London Stock Exchange. They doubtless returned handsomely.

The racist vein can be followed, disfiguring all of Thackeray's fiction after *Vanity Fair*. In *Henry Esmond* (1852), the hero and his wife finish as happy-ever-after slave owners in eighteenth-century Virginia. In *The Newcomes* (1855), we have Rummun Loll, the Indian swindler with a sinister taste for European women. In *The Virginians* (1859), drawing directly on the American experience of his lecture tour, there is Gumbo, at best a subhuman clown, at worst a liar and poltroon. And in the last complete novel, *Philip* (1862), a prominent role is given to Captain Woolcomb, the 'mulatto' dandy who steals Agnes from the blue-eyed hero of the title. When this odious 'blackamoor' stands for Parliament, 'manly' Englishman Philip Firmin speaks rousingly against him:

'If the two men', bawled Philip from the Ram window, 'could decide the contest with their coats off before the market-house yonder, which do you think would win – the fair man or the darkey? ... Are you men? Are you Englishmen? Are you white slaves to be sold to that fellow?'

One could call up a large number of similar momentary glimpses of where Thackeray stood on race. None of them reflect well on him.

He died very rich and built himself a fine mansion in his beloved Queen Anne-style at 2 Palace Green, Kensington. It is the kind of house the National Trust looks after and – as it has with Rudyard Kipling's Bateman's – deplores. But it is not the trust's to do so and probably never will be. Thackeray's great house, one of his proudest creations, is now the London Israeli Embassy. Given Thackeray's antisemitism, it is one of 'Life's Little Ironies', to borrow Thomas Hardy's term.

As said, I love Thackeray's fiction and have spent many years of my scholarly career working on it and on him. But I do not now love everything he wrote or its suppurating stain on the mass of his fiction. But why didn't I say so at the time? Or had I Victorianised myself to the extent that I simply did not see it?

My grandparents were arrantly racist and antisemitic in their attitudes. I imbibed it with the oversweet tea and over-buttered toast. It was part of their Kiplingesque pride in being British: one of the few claims to eugenic superiority they had. Was I, am I, still in some dark cellars of my being, unregenerate? Victorian?

It is too easy, I think, to say, as I have already several times, '*autres temps, autres mœurs*': the Victorians had their ways, and we have ours. Nor would one go so far with Thackeray as the editor of *Huckleberry Finn*, discussed above, who has, for the purpose of teaching Twain's novel to mixed-race classes, published his version sanitised of the Twain's time's casual racisms.

But what then does one do? Look shiftily the other way and not bring the subject up? Trigger the texts? I'm not sure that works with racism so inherent as Thackeray's. My hunch is that, without anyone saying much about it, Thackeray will slowly sink into oblivion, the Grimpen Mire that swallows most of published English literature and the existence of its overwhelmingly mayfly, 'books of the day'. Thackeray is even now well on the way to joining those millions of other forgotten authors whose works lie, gathering dust, as increasingly illegible tombstones gather lichen, in the vaults of the British Library. He is no longer important enough to trigger. A sad thought. I can finish here where I started; by pointing to what Kafka is quoted as saying in the epigraph of this book. Literature matters: to us and what we make of our world. But make the right choices.